# NATURE'S
## PLAYGROUND

# NATURE'S
## PLAYGROUND
### ACTIVITIES, CRAFTS, AND GAMES TO
### ENCOURAGE CHILDREN TO GET OUTDOORS

**FIONA DANKS**

**JO SCHOFIELD**

CHICAGO REVIEW PRESS

For Connie, Dan, Edward, Hannah, and Jake
—and the natural explorer in us all

First published in the United States of
America in 2007 by
Chicago Review Press, Incorporated
814 North Franklin Street
Chicago, Illinois 60610

First published in 2005 by Frances Lincoln
Limited
4 Torriano Mews
Torriano Avenue
London NW5 2RZ
www.franceslincoln.com

Designed by Caroline de Souza
Printed in China
2 3 4 5 6 7 8 9

Disclaimer
Neither the author nor the publisher can
accept any legal responsibility or liability
for any harm arising from participating
in the activities and games described
in this book.

ISBN-13: 978-1-55652-723-4
ISBN-10: 1-55652-723-3

ntents

# LET'S GET OUTDOORS

# NATURAL PLAYGROUNDS

Imagine children climbing high among the spreading branches of an ancient tree or damming a tumbling stream with sticks and stones. Imagine them crafting bows and arrows deep in the woods or watching in wonder as a crumpled dragonfly emerges from its nymph case. This is play in the great outdoors—imaginary games, exciting adventures, and amazing discoveries. The natural world is a place for exploration, learning about risk, building confidence, and escaping into the imagination. This book encourages adults and children to appreciate and enjoy wild places together and, above all, to have fun in the freedom of the great outdoors.

> Treat the earth well. It was not given to you by your parents, it was loaned to you by your children.
> *Native American proverb*

Sunshine pours invitingly through the window, and a commitment-free day stretches ahead. Outside, the leaves on the trees are unfurling in the spring sunshine, the first swallows swoop and dive, and the nearby pond is a mass of wriggling tadpoles. Indoors, listless children lounge around watching cartoons on TV, playing computer games, and squabbling over nothing. A bit of fresh air and exercise would do them the world of good, but the cheerful suggestion of a walk is greeted with howls of complaint and whines of "I'm too tired." Does this strike a familiar chord? Does it remind you of days when it seems as though nothing on earth will persuade fractious children to turn off the TV, pull on their boots, and get outside?

The good news is that it doesn't have to be like this. Imagine if the tables were turned and exuberant children were dragging you out for an adventure. They might want to build a secret den and try out their survival skills, construct tiny homes for elves, or look for creatures lurking in a pond. They might want to search for natural treasures, collecting leaves and seeds to create a magic carpet or gathering baskets of wild fruits for a pie. If every trip outdoors involved a daring expedition or a new discovery, then children would be pleading to go out—to finish their den, climb another tree, or look for more tadpoles.

Given the opportunity, children will discover wonder and excitement outdoors. Yet all too often, adults walk straight through wild places dragging the children along behind them. By taking time to stop and explore, you will make expeditions much more fun for everyone. This book encourages families to take the outdoor experience a little further, to become immersed in the natural world, to let their imagination take flight. A walk across the pasture may become a dangerous hunt for dinosaurs (otherwise known as lizards) basking in the sun; a stroll past a pond might turn into a game to race boats made from twigs and rushes. And not every minute of every day needs to be filled with noise and busyness. Children also enjoy quiet times in special places, lying in long grass surrounded by chirping crickets, or lounging on sunny rocks watching the comings and goings of a tidal rockpool.

Playing outdoors should be a fundamental part of childhood, yet we are in danger of tidying our children away into stuffy bedrooms . . .

Many parents and grandparents share childhood memories of endless days of freedom, days when they were packed off in the morning and not expected home until suppertime. They didn't have computer games, mobile phones, personal stereos, or the Internet—they just had friends and went outside to play together. Today the nature of childhood has changed, and many grandparents look on in alarm at a materialistic generation over-burdened with plastic toys but without enough opportunities to pursue their own imaginations.

Playing outdoors should be a fundamental part of childhood, but we are in danger of tidying our children away into stuffy bedrooms packed with electronic tranquillizers. Children's charities believe that every child should have the right to play safely near the home, yet their research reveals that children are often prevented from playing outside by intolerant adults, who accuse them of causing a nuisance or making too much noise. As the lives of children become more and more sedentary there are growing concerns about the increased incidence of childhood obesity and other related physical and emotional health problems.

Yet the natural world still provides a playground, a place for unsophisticated, unstructured, healthy fun. Not far from my family's home a spring gushes out of the ground, filling an overgrown pond and flowing away along a streambed. Twelve-year-old

Edward and his friends have spent many happy hours there, scrambling along the branches of the surrounding willow trees, building dens and searching for frogs and newts. They do their own thing and they make their own adventures.

In the great outdoors, families can have fun without spending money on expensive toys or theme parks. Children can play and learn on their own initiative, following their own interests and enthusiasms. Exploring their environment from an early age helps children turn into inquisitive adults who want to know more about the world. Of course we want our children to grow up computer-literate and equipped with all the skills they need to survive in the modern world, but a balance should be struck. Children need to learn how to use the tools of the twenty-first century without losing their innate love and respect for wild places.

wild places and ourselves, and provide children with opportunities to reconnect with nature. Young children have a real affinity with the natural world, an insatiable curiosity, and a sense of wonder about the tiniest details. They will stare in awe at a ladybug crawling along a stem or crouch down to investigate a disciplined army of ants carrying bits of leaf back to their nest. They will blow dandelion clocks, counting the time or chanting, "he loves me, he loves me not," as they watch the parachute seeds fly away.

Just being outdoors releases children's natural exuberance and sends them running through the wind, rolling down grassy slopes, paddling up streams, turning cartwheels on the beach, or dancing barefoot in the rain. Once out there they should have the motivation and the imagination to play, but they will still need responsible adults with the time and energy to take them—and a few activities tucked up their sleeves.

If you are a parent, grandparent, uncle or aunt, godparent, caregiver, babysitter, play-leader or teacher—if you have some responsibility for children through your family or your work—this book can provide both the inspiration and the practical ideas to help you explore wild places together. The most important thing is to share in a child's joy and excitement, whether they have discovered a butterfly or an earthworm, a bird's feather or a rabbit's skull.

Unfortunately, many children grow up alienated from wild places, wary of the countryside because it lacks the hard edges of "civilization." In our headlong rush to embrace change and "progress," our lives grow further and further away from natural rhythms, and some people seem anxious to keep all wild things at bay. The lives of ancient peoples were completely intertwined with natural cycles; they recognized they were an integral part of the world and knew how to use it without abusing it. Today the only daily contact many people have with the natural world is feeling the heat of the sun or the wetness of the rain, yet our lives still depend on nature's rhythms.

If tomorrow's caretakers of the earth are to love and understand the natural world, they need to explore it, enjoy it, and recognize our reliance upon it. We have to peel away all those layers between

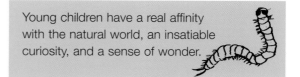

Young children have a real affinity with the natural world, an insatiable curiosity, and a sense of wonder.

# BEING MORE ADVENTUROUS

Ghastly images filled our minds as we raced through the woods, searching frantically for our missing sons. During a long walk with several families a whole gang of children had run on ahead, but my twelve-year-old and a friend's six-year-old had taken the wrong path and become separated from the others. They had been missing for about twenty-five minutes before we even realized what had happened. We must have run for half a mile before we spotted the two boys ambling along together. Our relieved hugs were casually shrugged off, as they chattered excitedly about their adventure. The younger boy had looked for help to the older, who had risen to the challenge; they retraced their steps and worked out where they had gone wrong. Although we shouldn't have let it happen, the experience had given something valuable to both boys.

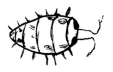

As parents and caregivers, we are responsible for the health and safety of children, but this doesn't mean we should cosset them in completely risk-free surroundings. In today's increasingly litigious, safety-conscious society, when even the school nature table is considered a potential health hazard, youngsters are not encouraged to go off and play in the local woods or park for fear of accidents, traffic, or abduction. Many parents prefer to keep their children indoors, glued to the TV or game station; they aren't against their children going outside but are frightened of letting them do so. While these fears may be very real, young people want and need opportunities to play outdoors. We should face up to the fact that certain risks are exaggerated through extensive media coverage, and try to equip our children to cope with the outside world.

Life is full of risk, so the best way to prepare children for life is to ensure that they understand how to judge risk for themselves.

Young animals find out about survival by playing with each other in potentially dangerous situations, gradually getting bolder and extending boundaries. Life is full of risk, so the best way to prepare children for life is to ensure that they understand how to judge risk for themselves. Of course wild places can be hazardous—there are things that bite, scratch, and sting, there are things that must not be eaten, there is water to fall into, trees and rocks to fall off, and woods to get lost in— but this is no reason to stop children from going there. Try to provide them with the knowledge they need to stay safe: children taught how to whittle and carve with a penknife are less likely to cut themselves than a child who hasn't a clue.

By encouraging parents and caregivers to explore the natural world with their children, this book aims to help families to become a little more adventurous and stop parents feeling guilty about letting go. Exploring nature with children may mean joining in wholeheartedly with their games and adventures—hiding in the long grass and making mud pies—or it may involve sitting on the sidelines, allowing the youngsters some space and freedom, and letting them make a few mistakes. If they graze a knee, cut a finger on a rough piece of grass, or stand on a sharp thorn with bare feet, it will help them learn to be more careful next time. The important thing is to be waiting somewhere in the wings, ready to intervene if necessary, and make sure no real harm comes to them. Some basic safety tips can be found on page 186.

# SOMETHING FOR EVERYONE

Whether you and your young friends have scientific or creative minds or lively imaginations, whether the children need to let off steam or take a little time out, or whether you want to share a family walk or explore a new place together, we hope there will be something in this book for you. A wide range of activities have been included, falling into five broad categories that encourage children to make discoveries, have adventures, use their imaginations, be creative, and use all their senses.

**Making discoveries** You will find that young children have an immense curiosity about the natural world—the challenge is to stop them from losing it! Nurture that precious sense of wonder and direct it to help children discover for themselves what lives under the stones in the garden or in the rockpools at the beach. Rather than just supplying them with secondhand facts, allow them the space to make their own discoveries. A little empathy and enthusiasm is all

> To fully appreciate the diversity of nature, we need to explore it in as many different ways as we can.

you need to encourage children to appreciate wild places; an in-depth knowledge of natural history is not necessary. For those children who do want to go on and find out more, there are many good reference books available and wildlife clubs to join.

**Having adventures** Nature provides exciting playgrounds where children can balance, climb, jump, swing, and hide. A patch of woodland might become a dangerous forest to be explored by brave adventurers armed to the teeth or an outlaw's hideaway to be protected by Robin Hood and his Merry Men. All natural environments can offer opportunities for adventures, surprises, and experiences that will help to build a child's confidence and instill bravery.

**Using their imagination** Allow children time to become completely immersed in their games, so that nothing can spoil their imaginings. Wherever they are they will adapt natural materials, weaving them intricately into secret worlds of their own where adults cannot follow. Some children may need a little prod to spark their imaginations: perhaps catkins dropped from a hazel tree could become

prefer to collect feathers or autumn leaves to take home and make into something for keeps.

By using natural materials creatively we begin to appreciate them in new and varied ways. A stick may no longer be just any old stick, but a stick that's the perfect length and color to finish a pattern. A dismantled dandelion might provide the raw materials for a collage. A shell on the beach might turn out to be exactly the right shape to complete a mosaic in the sand.

**Using all their senses** Wild places also provide opportunities for quiet reflective experiences. To fully appreciate the diversity of nature, we need to explore it in as many different ways as we can. Try encouraging children to forget their eyes and give all the other senses a chance. They might sample the scents of herbs and flowers, taste wild blackberries, find a special place to sit and listen to natural sounds, or put on a blindfold and explore a mossy tree stump with their fingertips. This book includes a range of activities that help to increase sensory awareness of the environment, making time for feeling, smelling, tasting, and listening as well as seeing.

caterpillars in search of a home; a pile of pebbles, a ruined castle; someone else's abandoned den, a hero's hideout . . . You could also use a favorite book or film as the starting point of a game, the children taking on the roles of the characters.

**Being creative** Mud, sand, and ice can be molded and shaped; sticks and stones can be used to create towers and sculptures; shells, leaves, petals, and seeds can be made into collages, mobiles, or decorations. Try not to use any man-made materials at all—perhaps thorns could be used as pins, grasses as string or water, and mud as glue. Children might create something out in the woods or on the beach and go back a few days later to see the effects of time and the elements, or they might

# TIPS FOR SHARING WILD PLACES

The activities in this book can be enjoyed by families or groups in a wide variety of settings and at different times of year. The following tips may be helpful whenever you are exploring nature's playground together.

- The caregiver's role is to encourage. Let the children's enthusiasm drag you in and perhaps they will help you to rediscover some of the magic of your own childhood.

- Let the children help to plan the expedition around a specific goal. Children like to feel involved in planning an outing.

- Be prepared to drop the original plan if something better turns up. So many children's lives are tightly scheduled, moving from one organized activity to another. Instead, allow them to follow a spontaneous course, developing a game on the spur of the moment if it feels right. It doesn't matter if a pond-dipping expedition becomes a session making rush boats or if they come across a tree begging to be climbed or a mossy log they just have to investigate.

- Team up with others. Children love to go exploring with a gang of friends.

- Remember that there is always something interesting going on in wild places—it's just a case of finding it.

- Always look at the little as well as the big things.

- Why wait until summertime? Take children out all year round so they find out more about the earth's natural cycles. Revisit places to see how they change with the seasons.

- Give children the space to make their own discoveries and when the questions start to come, seek the answers together. Don't worry about not knowing names.

- Let children become completely immersed in nature. Allow them to get soaked to the skin in a summer rainstorm or plastered from head to foot in mud; let them stain their hands and arms with blackberry juice or have play fights with newly mown grass. Give them the freedom to muck about, get dirty, and generally have fun.

- Nature can be cruel—it is, after all, about survival of the fittest. Don't hide this from children. They will see signs of predation—a bloody clump of bird's feathers, a diving beetle sucking the life out of a tadpole, or a much-loved dog proudly dropping a dead rabbit at their feet. Help them to understand that each species has to find its own way to survive.

- Don't let the children become very noisy and over-excited; they might disturb wildlife or spoil the enjoyment of other people.

- Enthusiasm may sometimes need containing or even redirecting—but never squashing. Some years ago, during a very wet walk round a nature reserve, one young boy discovered that the rain had enticed masses of large black slugs out of their usual hiding places. Tearing off his T-shirt, he

began to stick slugs all over his chest until he was plastered with a slimy, slithery black mess. We all watched in amazement and even horror, yet nobody tried to stifle his enthusiasm. At the end of the walk he returned the slugs lovingly to the undergrowth. (I often wonder how this particular enthusiasm was redirected!)

- Don't expect it all to be easy. There will of course be times when the children get tired, argue, whine, and want to go home, but it is amazing what a little coaxing and a few treats can do. On one trip, the children took one look at the huge hill we expected them to climb and announced they were too tired. But with encouragement and a little bribery they reached the summit, where they gazed in awe at the rolling countryside laid out like patchwork below.

- Always remember to treat your environment with respect and try to leave each place as you found it. Help children to enjoy exploring wild places without damaging the delicate balance of nature.

- Don't lead the children—let them lead you.

# WHERE TO GO

Some of the most-visited destinations in the world are those treasured for their natural beauty and grandeur. Whether they are high mountain ranges or unspoiled coastlines these places can offer an escape from a busy world. But there is no need to venture out into the wilderness to find true wildness. Try looking in the long grass at the bottom of the garden, among the trees at the park, or in the hedge beside a local footpath. Some of the activities described in this book are most suitable for the woods, the coast, or a remote national park, but others are ideal for the parks and gardens of urban areas—such sites offer surprisingly rich habitats.

Unless you have been given specific permission to use an area of private land, only explore places where there is public access. These might include:

- Beaches

- National parks

- Nature reserves

- Managed forests and arboretums

- Common land

- Country parks. These countryside spaces, set aside for recreation, are often found on the edges of built-up areas.

- Horse trails and footpaths. Rights of way are often bordered by hedges and areas of undisturbed grassland and scrub. Not only do they provide important wildlife habitats in their own right but they also act as corridors linking together larger wild places.

- Country lanes and tracks/disused railway lines. These places may also offer unspoiled shoulders and thick hedges.

- Playing fields and recreation grounds. Although

such sites are closely mown for sport, they may be surrounded by trees and hedges and retain corners of wildness.

- Urban open spaces. These might include parks, riverbanks, and canalsides. Make sure that there is safe public access.

- Gardens and school grounds. Many of the activities are suitable for these areas, particularly if a little wildness has been allowed to creep in.

- See the list of organizations and Web sites on page 189 for more information about ways of finding wild places.

# WHAT TO TAKE

Successful explorers are always properly prepared and equipped, ready to cope with every eventuality. This may seem a little over the top for a walk up the road, but you never know what children may discover or what might grab their imaginations. Whether you are hoping to climb a mountain, build a den in the woods, or simply visit the canal at the end of the street, it is good to be ready for anything. Suitable clothes and an adventure bag containing treats and useful items such as bug boxes and a sieve will keep children happy in all weathers.

## CLOTHES

Everyone should wear practical, comfortable clothes; avoid those cool jeans or that new T-shirt. It is a shame if an exciting adventure is ruined because some favorite clothes are ripped on a bramble or

stained by berries, so encourage children to wear old ones. Take along a few spares, just in case the weather changes or someone falls in a stream. For further information about suitable seasonal clothing, see "Ready for summer" (page 65) and "Ready for winter" (page 117).

## FOOTWEAR

Footwear should also be comfortable and practical, such as old sneakers, rainboots, or walking boots. When it comes to mud, puddles, and streams, rain boots are the best option, but for longer outings and tree climbing, children may prefer a pair of stout, well-fitting boots with good ankle support.

## FIRST-AID KIT

It is always a good idea to carry a small first-aid kit. A bandage on a cut or a little cream dabbed on a sting works wonders with distressed children! Your first-aid kit might include:

• Bandages for minor cuts, grazes, and blisters

• Antiseptic cream for keeping minor wounds clean

• Antihistamine cream for insect stings and bites

• Arnica for bruising

• High-factor sunscreen

## REFRESHMENTS

Young children can run out of energy quite suddenly. No matter how long your expedition might be, take along some drinks and a few snacks. If youngsters start to get tired or lose interest, find a nice place to stop for a little rest and a picnic.

- Take plenty of drinking water. This will also be useful for washing hands or cuts.

- Always include carbohydrate-based snacks. Sweets provide instant energy, but the carbohydrates found in foods such as bread or cereal bars provide more sustained energy.

- Take fresh and dried fruit such as apples, bananas, and dried raisins and apricots.

- Chocolate and sweets are very popular with children when they are out exploring, but try to encourage them to fill up on healthier foods and keep the sugary things to offer as occasional treats and rewards.

## ADVENTURE BAG

Tucked away under our stairs is an old knapsack, always ready to be taken out on expeditions at a moment's notice. This is our adventure bag, packed with useful things for helping us to explore the natural world. An adventure bag might contain:

- Magnifying glasses

- Bug boxes (perspex boxes with a magnifying lid are ideal for collecting and watching invertebrates)

- Plastic boxes/bowls/bags for examining wildlife and storing collections of materials

- Old paintbrushes for gently lifting wildlife finds

- Sieves for pond or stream dipping

- Old gloves (preferably gardening gloves)

- Eye-shades/scarves for playing blindfold games

- String

- Penknife

- Water bottle

- Notebook and pencils/pens

- Basic first-aid kit

- Whistle

- Other useful items might include a camera and a pair of binoculars.

Some families may wish to take along a walkie-talkie set or a couple of mobile phones, but it is a mistake to rely too heavily on these.

# ENCOURAGING CHILDREN TO WALK

New parents who are enthusiastic walkers find their hobby remains relatively unchanged as long as the baby fits snugly into a backpack, but once a child grows bigger and heavier life takes on a slower pace and the adult stride must be shortened to suit little legs. Yet despite what many parents believe, it is possible for young children to complete and even enjoy quite long walks. The expectations of the adults may need to change, and the routes may have to be planned more carefully, but it can be done.

Wherever you walk, children will have very different expectations than the grown-ups. We are happy simply to get the exercise and fresh air, to enjoy the scenery and some company, but most children need a more hands-on experience. Not content with just passing through, they want to stop and take a closer look.

My daughter Hannah climbed her first mountain in blistering heat at the age of five. We chose an accessible peak, with a short walk up a glen followed by a steep climb and some rock scrambling to the summit. We helped her along by looking out for plants and insects, singing songs, and finding little gifts left by the sweetie fairy. Once on the rocks she rose to the challenge of working out her own route, reaching the summit triumphantly to see a whole island laid out below.

During the descent she swam in a mountain stream and stroked a slow-worm which her grandfather had found. The experience left her exhausted but with a huge sense of achievement and a desire to see more of the mountains.

Such walks are even possible in winter. Jo and her family stayed in a camping barn one February, hoping to introduce Jake, Dan, and Connie to the mountains. At first they wondered if their plan was unrealistic, even irresponsible, but equipped with warm clothes, stout boots, plentiful supplies, a first-aid kit, and a good map they set off on a crisp clear morning in search of adventure. The children became hobbits escaping from the Dark Riders, their imaginations running riot. The game kept everyone on the move—and before they knew it the children had reached the summit.

Whether you are walking in mountains, by the coast, through fields and woods, or in a park, each outing can become a game, an expedition, or an imaginary quest. If they are flexible and prepared to play along, the adults may be surprised by just how far their children can walk and how much fun the whole family can get out of the experience.

Not content with just passing through, children want to stop and take a closer look.

## PLANNING THE ROUTE

I know full well that a long trudge around plowed fields or across a bleak plain would not appeal to my children. When planning a walk, think from the children's perspective. Will there be some trees to climb, a stream to play in, some rocks to scramble over, or a woodland dell where you can have a picnic? If you want your children to return from a walk asking for more, make sure it is fun, exciting, and even challenging.

**A varied route** Choose a combination of paths that cross a range of habitats. If you are aiming to climb a hill, you could perhaps select a route that begins in woodland, crosses a meadow, runs alongside a stream, and finishes with a scramble up to the summit. A path that twists and turns is likely to appeal to young walkers; they will never know what might be lurking around the next corner ...

**A challenging route** Children often prefer a narrow, winding path to a broad, straight one and stepping-stones across a stream to a bridge. They love to clamber over boulders and run up and down sand dunes. Scrambling up a steep, rocky path is much more satisfying than plodding up a gentle slope; children enjoy the challenge of looking for the next handhold and working out where to put their feet.

**A circular route** This is more rewarding for everyone. It is always a bit demoralizing to turn around and go back the same way you came.

**Get them planning too** Involve the children in choosing and planning the route. Look at the map with them and discuss which way to go. They may decide to return to a walk they have done before, to make repairs to a den or visit a favorite climbing tree.

**Be flexible** Don't set off with just one route in mind; have some alternatives up your sleeve. Be prepared to respond to things that grab the children's attention—let them stop to investigate finds such as a pool full of newts or a lizard basking in the sun.

**Think little** The sensation of being on top of the world does not have to involve scaling the heights of Ben Nevis, the Matterhorn, or the Rocky Mountains. Start off with something much smaller, a hill or even a rocky outcrop that stands alone and above the surrounding area. Call it your child's first mountain, and let them experience that wonderful top-of-the-world feeling.

**Think slow** The distance you achieve is immaterial. It is the enjoyment of being outdoors that matters.

The richness of the natural world is revealed only if you take the time to find it. Little children love to stop to look for beetles under logs and crickets in the grass or to watch ducklings swim across a pond.

**Have a target in mind** This might be the top of a mountain, a beach, or a lakeshore, where you could perhaps have a picnic or stop to play for a while. It is important to set realistic targets, taking into account the speed at which your children walk. It may be worthwhile thinking of a second, less ambitious target in case the first one should prove impossible.

**Make your walk into an expedition** A walk is an opportunity to discover something—an island, perhaps, or a mountain fort. Visit somewhere that the children can relate to in some way, perhaps through a favorite book or film. You might go in search of Max and the Wild Things (from *Where the Wild Things Are*) in a forest, look out for Toad and Ratty (from *Wind in the Willows*) along a riverbank, or search for Little Bear (from *Blueberries for Sal*) on a hillside.

## PACKING FOR WALKS

Although equipment and supplies have already been covered in "What to take" (page 22), here are a few extra tips for long walks:

**Take a map and perhaps a compass** These are always worth bringing unless you are very familiar with the terrain.

**Pack a few surprises** Ideas for activities and some tasty treats will restore energy when needed.

**Get the children to be real explorers** Let them pack their own knapsacks with food and drink, a compass and map, string, some money, a collecting bag, and a magnifying glass. (The only drawback is that you may end up carrying their adventure bags when they start to get tired!)

**Respect wild places** Remember that conditions can change very quickly, particularly in the mountains. Keep an eye on the weather forecast before you go, and be ready for anything by packing warm clothes and rain gear along with a hat and sun block.

## KEEPING THEM GOING

Once you have planned your route, and got everyone equipped and out the door, there are all sorts of ways and means to keep children walking and enjoying themselves.

**Sweetie fairy** This is the ideal way to encourage little walkers. An adult sneaks ahead every now and then to hide sweets on the route, perhaps placing them on a post, tree stump, or rock, or hanging them from twigs. Toddlers and young children love the excitement of searching for treats, eagerly following the path in search of the next place the sweetie fairy might have visited.

**Following a trail** This might be an established nature trail with dots or arrows, or a "do-it-yourself trail" when someone goes ahead to lay arrows on the ground using flour or natural materials such as twigs or stones. While looking for the arrows on the floor, youngsters may spot other things, such as animal tracks in the mud.

**Hide-and-seek** In this game a couple of people, including an adult, go to hide in a place where they can be seen from the path by observant seekers. The rest of the party follow the path looking for whoever is hiding. Make sure you are all agreed about which path you are following, otherwise the hiders could be waiting for a very long time!

**Walking the dog** If you don't have a dog, you can always borrow one. A dog will provide another focus for a walk, another playmate—and may even help to pull little children uphill.

**Walking with others** If two or more families meet up to go for a walk, the children will happily

stride along or run with their friends, perhaps teaming up to spy on each other and the grown-ups. The Parent-Teachers Association (PTA) of our local school organizes a family walk every spring, inviting people to join them on a planned route. Always a popular event, it even attracts families who don't usually go for walks, and whose children happily complete the five-mile route through the local countryside.

**Collecting games** All sorts of collecting games might be played on a walk, making use of whatever can be found. On one walk the children discovered a snail shell that a bird had broken on a rock, and they spent the next mile or so looking for more. This experience also inspired other collecting games, including one competition to see who could find the most slugs. Some collected items might be suitable for taking home to use in art and craft: a necklace could be created from empty snail shells, for example, or a mobile from fir cones and feathers.

**Alphabet games** Collecting games do not have to involve making a physical collection; spotting natural things beginning with each letter of the alphabet is a real challenge for the whole family.

**Role-play** Encourage children to make the walk more interesting by using ideas from whatever the latest favorite book or film might be. Young children may pretend the path is a railway track and they are Thomas the Tank Engine. Older children could be journeying hobbits, or Harry Potter venturing into the forest with Hagrid, or homesteaders from *Little House on the Prairie* . . .

**Using natural materials** Long leaves can become rabbit ears; forked twigs, reindeer antlers; feathers,

an Indian head-dress. Provided with wings of leaves, lagging children soon become birds, their tiredness disappearing as they swoop and flap along the track.

**Playing with sticks** Some children just like sticks for what they are, others pretend they are guns, flagpoles, walking sticks, or magic wands. It doesn't matter, as long as they provide a happy distraction and encourage the children to walk.

**Gathering food** Always take a container on late-summer or autumn walks; you might find raspberries in the woods, blueberries on a hillside, or blackberries in the hedges. Perhaps you could suggest that the berries are magical, with special powers to make children walk better. Avoid harvesting food from plants near roads, and make sure you know exactly what you are collecting.

**Painting and sketching** Pack some paper, paints, and pencils in your kit bag; some children enjoy stopping in a special place to make a painting or a drawing. It helps them to see wild places in different ways, looking more carefully at colors and shapes.

**Leading the way** When your energy is flagging, there is nothing worse than trailing along behind everyone else. Don't let a child get despondent at the rear; encourage him or her to lead the way instead. Perhaps the grown-ups could complain of being tired—lagging children may suddenly find the energy to pull them along!

**Setting the pace** Initial enthusiasm may wane if children start to run out of energy. Bear in mind how far you are walking and set a realistic pace.

**Spotting the photograph** Those who have a little time to plan ahead could provide the children with a series of photographs of features along the route and ask them to try to identify where each shot was taken.

**Map-reading** Let a child look at the map and find the way for a while. Help identify landmarks and perhaps allow mistakes to be made—there is probably another route you could take anyway.

**Varying the time of day** Why walk only in the afternoon? Try an early-morning walk to hear the dawn chorus or an evening walk to watch the sunset and look out for bats, owls, or glowworms.

The ideas described above are just a few suggestions that might help to make walking more fun for children. The rest of the book is not so much about walking from A to B, but rather about all the adventures to be had if you make a little time to stop on the way.

# SPRING

# MAKING THE MOST OF SPRING

Every season and each time of day has its wonders—the mysterious toadstools of autumn and the sparkling snow of winter, the dawn chorus of spring and the swooping bats of a summer's night. Yet the progression of nature's changes has little direct relevance to the lives of many people. The seasons may slip by largely unremarked, until one day we notice that the daffodils are out in the park or the apples are ripening in the garden. Sometimes the seasons are marked by more sudden and dramatic changes—a hard freeze, strong winds ripping leaves off the trees, or a heavy rain overfilling rivers. Some of the most memorable outdoor experiences can take place during times of sudden change in weather, such as the unexpected thunderstorms of summer or the swiftly alternating radiant sunshine and heavy showers of spring.

Children notice seasonal change if only because the longer days and warmer weather of summer give them more freedom, while winter means more time cooped up indoors. But nature's playground has attractions all year round, and many of the games and activities in this book focus on seasonal characteristics—the new life of spring, the abundance of summer, the decay of autumn, or the dormancy of winter. In reality, however, one season merges seamlessly with the next; the musty scent of autumn is detected in the air long before we are ready for summer to end, and snowdrops burst out of the ground in search of light during the depths of winter.

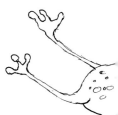

Seasonal change is perhaps most eagerly awaited in spring, when increasing temperatures and hours of daylight bring about startling transformations. This is a season of firsts—the first clouds of blossom, the first green shoots, the first swallow. Woodland floors burst into life early in the year, making the most of the light before the trees overhead come into leaf. Then the waiting buds on seemingly lifeless twigs begin to open; fed by the sun's energy the tightly compacted leaves are able to unfurl and grow. Catkins of birch, alder, and hazel stretch out to become the dangling flowers sometimes called lambs' tails. Children often notice the soft silvery buds of pussy willow, but perhaps they can also spot other early tree flowers, such as the startling red flowers of the larch or the dainty scarlet flowers of the hazel.

Spring's sunshine brings out those animals that have lain low or hibernated over winter. Children might look for insects emerging from their winter's

rest; butterflies, bees, and ladybugs crawl out of hiding places to soak up the sunshine. Birds that spent the winter in warmer climes begin to return to feed on the increasingly abundant insect life. Lizards can be seen lying on stones or piles of logs, basking in the sun until they warm up enough to catch their prey. Frogs and toads wake from their sleep, heading off in search of ponds where they will mate and produce their jelly-like spawn.

We too feel a greater urge to get outside, shed the winter layers, feel the first warm rays of sunshine on our skin, and enjoy the longer days. Take the children out for an early spring walk to look and listen for different signs of spring. Try going into the woods at dusk; the undergrowth is not yet dense and hibernation is ending, so this is the best time of year to look for mammals in the wild. Or just go out in search of surprises.

# BOWS AND ARROWS

Whether children are being hobbits or elves tearing through the woods in search of orks, or Robin Hood and his gang of outlaws lying in wait to ambush a passing carriage, a proper bow and arrow will bring their imaginary adventures to life. A working bow and arrow adds a tingling sense of excitement and even danger to a game—this is definitely an activity that requires careful supervision, and children must be shown how to play safely.

Making bows and arrows is always popular on a family walk or at an outdoor children's party. The children might want to protect themselves from imaginary enemies or practice aiming at a target chalked on a tree trunk or an apple stuck on a fence post. And best of all they get to take their very own bow and arrow home with them, to be used over and over again. They will be able to take their bow out on every expedition, so that even a short walk around the nearby park becomes a mission to capture some unsuspecting foe.

Although bows and arrows can be made at any time of year, the rising sap of spring ensures the strongest, most flexible bows. Look for the slender stems of hazel found commonly in hedges and woods. Cutting hazel right back to its base encourages the growth of straight new shoots; this traditional method of woodland management, called coppicing, produces a crop of supple stems for making fencing stakes and furniture. Hazel coppicing has undergone something of a revival in recent years, enriching woodland habitats, and the flexible poles produced are the perfect material for making bows that are both supple and strong.

**YOU WILL NEED**
- String
- Cotton thread
- A sharp knife

## MAKING THE BOWS

Making an effective bow is not easy. Young children will need adult help, particularly when cutting the wood and tensioning the bow.

- Select a living stem and bend it to check it is both flexible and strong. If making several bows, avoid cutting any more living stems than is absolutely necessary.

- Cut the stem to the required length, adjusting it to the size of the child. Short bows are safer as they have less power and may be preferable if working with several children. They perform just as well and are easier to use.

- Carve notches about ¾ inch (2 cm) from each end. These will help to fix the bowstring in place. There is no need to cut a notch if you use a forked stem, as the fork itself can be used to secure the string.

- Attach the string around one notch, or the fork, using a slipknot.

- Pull the string tight so the bow forms a wide arc. Tension the string by wrapping its loose end a couple of times around the other notch, securing it with a strong knot.

• Ensure the knots are tight and secure so the bow does not spring out of position.

## MAKING THE ARROWS

• For arrows use thin, straight sticks, such as dead sticks collected from the ground or slender lengths of willow or hazel with the bark removed.

• Flights made from split feathers add authenticity. Cut a 3-inch (8-cm) section of feather, and tear some of the long barbs off each end of the quill, leaving whole a central section of about 1½ inch (4 cm). Split the feather in half along the quill to create two sections. Place one section on either side of the end of the arrow, and fix them in place by winding cotton thread around the sections and the arrow, securing with a knot.

• Children can make their own quivers for carrying arrows by looping a length of string through a long cardboard tube and sealing one end with tape.

### SAFETY TIPS
• Always supervise children when they are using knives.
• Adult help is essential when tensioning the bow.
• Bows and arrows should be used with care, under adult supervision.
• Never aim arrows at people or animals.
• Make sure all children have laid down their bows before any go to collect their arrows.

# TWIG SCULPTURES

The ancient art of willow-weaving has been given a new lease of life in recent years by sculptors who craft abstract shapes and animal figures from willow. When Jo and her family were out walking they spotted a beautiful woven deer grazing quietly in a woodland glade. It had been carefully crafted by an unknown sculptor and left in the woods for others to find and enjoy.

The discovery inspired Jake to try to make his own twig sculpture. Starting with four sturdy sticks stuck into the ground, he worked with his dad to weave and twist willow and hazel twigs to create a little deer. After some time and experimentation, they created a natural sculpture, which they left behind for others to discover.

**YOU WILL NEED**
- A sharp knife
- Old gardening gloves

**SAFETY TIP**
Children using knives should be supervised at all times.

## MAKING A TWIG SCULPTURE

During early spring, wood is bendy and pliable, making it easier to work. Use long, thin lengths of willow, hazel, or other shrubs, but do not cut large amounts of such materials from wild plants. This activity is ideal for a park or garden after a late-winter or early-spring pruning session, or can be done out in woods where there will be plenty of suitable material available. Try collecting as much dead material from the ground as possible, so that only a small amount of the more pliable living wood needs to be cut from the trees.

Children might like to try making an animal like a deer or a magical creature such as a dragon. Alternatively, they may prefer to try to create a basketlike structure, a nest, or a chair—the creative decision is up to them!

- Start off by using dead twigs and small branches to build the main supports and then weave around those.

- Use only natural materials. Grasses and lengths of honeysuckle or ivy can be used as binding where necessary.

- Although it is not difficult to make simple sculptures, the weaving does require considerable patience and cooperation; this is perhaps a challenge for older children or even adults.

# YOUR VERY OWN PLACE

Now and again we all need a breathing space. You can help children to find a special wild place of their own in which to observe their surroundings, safe in the knowledge that you are not far away. Even very lively children respond well to the opportunity to take some time out, and if they are patient and lucky they may even hear and see things that would be missed in the usual hullabaloo.

The natural world offers many special places for resting quietly. Children can try lying among bluebells or hiding between the roots of a beech tree, peering out at the woodland world beyond; or perhaps they could sit on the bank of a brook, watching for fish darting through the water. This activity encourages children to choose their own tiny kingdoms, somewhere they go on their own.

• Ask each member of the group to find a place to sit or lie quietly, within sight of an agreed meeting point. The children should each choose their own space—somewhere that appeals to them, where they can make themselves comfortable.

• For five minutes or longer everyone should stay as still as possible, watching and listening, trying to feel part of the surroundings. Children might observe details such as birds singing, a butterfly resting on a leaf, a beetle scurrying along the ground, or perhaps a squirrel leaping from branch to branch. If they are very quiet and patient they may be rewarded with close-up views of birds or other creatures.

• Pre-arrange a signal at which everyone will emerge from their special place and gather together to compare notes on what they have seen and heard.

• Children may like to return to the same place during future outings, to see how it changes as the year progresses.

• Try providing children with a cardboard picture frame and asking them to find their favorite view from the special place. How many colors, shapes, or living things can they see inside the frame?

• Children might like to paint or sketch something they can see from their chosen spot.

**SAFETY TIP**

Mark a central meeting point with a bag or coat, and explain that everyone must be able to see it from his or her special place. This should stop anyone from venturing too far away.

# POND AND STREAM DIPPING

Water is an irresistible magnet to children: they love to float things on it, paddle and splash, search for fish, and try to dam it. Exploring the underwater world and discovering the tiny creatures that live there is both exciting and intriguing. Life can be found in even the most unpromising trickle of a stream or muddy pond, whether in the shape of frogs and their tadpoles, pond skaters gliding over the water's surface, or the great variety of winged creatures, such as dragonflies, damselflies, and mayflies, that spend most of their lives submerged as nymphs. Pond and stream dipping brings together children of all ages, crowding around eagerly to look at their catch, sharing their delight in discovering the animals living in and near the water.

## CHOOSING A POND/STREAM

- Only use sites where there is public access, unless you have the owner's permission.

- Streams and ponds with clear water and plentiful marginal vegetation support the most wildlife.

- Make sure the children can safely dip their nets into the water without sliding or falling in. The banks of the pond or stream should shelve gently. Alternatively, you could visit a pond with a specially constructed dipping platform.

- Choose a spot where the banks are not too overgrown.

- Avoid sites with lots of litter or signs of pollution.

## BEFORE YOU START

Discovering the great variety of life in aquatic habitats requires a little patience as many of the animals are small and some are well camouflaged. Don't let children run noisily toward the water; encourage them to approach quietly and see if they can spot any signs of life. There may be birds drinking or hunting by the water's edge, frogs and toads lurking among the weeds, beetles whizzing

round dizzily on the surface, or fish swimming in the depths. Perhaps each child could find a place to sit near the water and watch for a few minutes before starting to explore further.

## HOW TO DIP

- Fill a large container and a couple of smaller containers with water from the pond or stream. Place these on level ground near the water's edge, ready to receive your catch.

- Ask the children to look carefully to see if they have caught something already. The water may be alive with miniature creatures such as water fleas.

- Now is the time to use the net or sieve. Move it slowly and gently through the water, close to marginal plants where animals may be sheltering. Try not to collect too much mud.

- Empty the net or sieve by gently turning it inside-out directly into the water of the largest container. Leave for a couple of minutes to allow any mud or silt to settle, then take a close look to see whether you have caught anything.

- Remind children to treat their catch very carefully and handle it as little as possible. Many of the creatures cannot survive for very long out of water.

- Using a paintbrush or spoon, transfer some of your catch to the cleaner water in a smaller container.

- Try rinsing pieces of weed into the container—animals may be hiding there.

- In shallow streams or ponds, carefully lift the stones and look underneath to see if any creatures, such as caddis fly larvae, are lurking there (always replace the stones as you found them).

- When you have finished, return all the water, plants, and creatures to where they were found, rinsing out the nets and containers carefully.

### YOU WILL NEED

- A net such as a seaside shrimping net or a homemade one (see the instructions on page 45). If you can get close to the water's edge, an old sieve works very well.
- Large containers, such as empty ice cream tubs or an old washing-up bowl
- Smaller containers, such as jam jars
- A bug box or magnifying glass
- Old paintbrushes and spoons
- A field guide (if you would like to try to identify your catch)

### SAFETY TIPS

- Wear shoes or boots with a non-slip sole.
- Ensure all cuts and scratches are completely covered with waterproof bandages.
- Only dip where there is safe access to the water from gently sloping banks or a sturdy platform.
- Always wash hands thoroughly with soap after pond or stream dipping.

Frog spawn

Baby tadpoles
in eggs

Baby tadpole

Growing tadpole

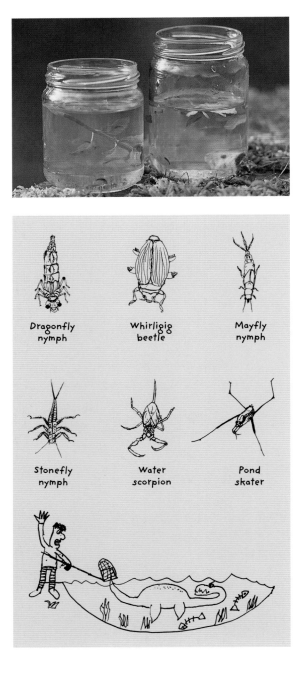

Dragonfly
nymph

Whirligig
beetle

Mayfly
nymph

Stonefly
nymph

Water
scorpion

Pond
skater

## THE CATCH MAY INCLUDE

**Water boatmen** So called because two of their legs are used like oars. Watch how they come up to the surface to collect bubbles of air.

**Diving beetles** These are fast-swimming beetles. Like the water boatmen they have no gills, but collect bubbles of air which they use much as a human diver uses a tank of oxygen.

**Dragonfly and damselfly nymphs** These fiercely predatory creatures spend most of their lives underwater, emerging as the more familiar winged adults in the spring and summer months.

**Mayfly nymphs** Generally smaller than damsel and dragonfly nymphs, mayfly nymphs feed on organic matter in ponds and streams. The adults only live for about one day and are not able to feed.

**Freshwater hoglouse** An aquatic version of the woodlouse.

**Freshwater shrimp** These common crustaceans are related to the brine shrimps, familiar to many children as "sea monkeys," a popular pet sold as eggs in toy shops.

Tadpole with
back legs

Froglet with tail

Froglet

Adult frog

**Water scorpion** Although this fearsome-looking creature resembles a scorpion, its tail is a hollow tube that is used, like a snorkel, for sucking in air from the surface.

**Tadpoles** Most commonly the youngsters of frogs, but also those of toads and newts. Many families love to take tadpoles home and watch them metamorphose. Although this is a wonderful thing to do, you must remember to return them to where you found them once they start to grow legs.

**Caddis fly larvae** Children might find these fascinating creatures hiding inside camouflaged cases, which protect them from predators and conceal them from their prey. Each species builds to its own particular pattern, perhaps using tiny stones and grains of sand or twigs or leaves, and sticks the case together with silk. Children can try to make their own caddis fly cases by rolling a piece of sticky tape around itself, sticky side out, then covering it in minute stones or leaves.

## MAKING A SMALL NET

This net is not very strong, but it is quick and easy to make.

- Cut off the feet and most of the legs of the tights and either tie together the remainder of the legs or sew them up to make a net shape.

- Bend the stick around to form a loop and secure it in place as shown (right).

- Wrap the waist of the tights around the loop a couple of times, securing in place with a few stitches if need be.

## MAKING A LARGER NET

This method produces a stronger net, but is a little more complicated (see photograph on page 42).

- Sew a wide hem (at least 1in/2.5cm) along one of the longer sides of the muslin.

- Fold the muslin in half, with the hemmed side positioned at the top as the opening, and then sew along the bottom and up the open side to create a net shape.

- Untwist the hanger and thread the wire all the way around inside the hem of the net. Twist the ends of the wire tightly together to secure them.

- Attach the wire ends to the broom handle using the jubilee clip. Any bits of wire sticking out should be tied to the broom handle with strong, waterproof tape or string.

### YOU WILL NEED

**SMALL NET**
- Old pair of tights
- Supple stick
- Needle and thread
- Scissors

**LARGE NET**
- Piece of muslin about 20 inch by 39 inch (50 cm × 1 m)
- Wire clothes hanger
- Jubilee clip (hose connection)
- Broom handle
- Strong waterproof tape/string
- Sewing machine/needle and thread

# BIRDS' NESTS

One spring holiday, Hannah and Edward decided to make some birds' nests. After collecting suitable nest-building materials while out on a family walk, they became absorbed in weaving flexible twigs of broom into cup shapes and lining each one with a soft bed of moss and lichen. They hid the nests in shrubs all around their grandparents' garden, where they remained for years, unoccupied but still complete. Their game reminded me of a passage in E. Nesbit's classic tale *The Railway Children*, in which two of the characters have a wonderful, muddy time making swallows' nests out of clay. Their plan is to dry them in the oven, line them with wool, and then hang them under the eaves ready for the swallows' arrival the following spring.

Nests provide shelter and warmth and, most importantly, a safe place where adult birds can lay and incubate eggs and rear their young. Some species build incredibly intricate, finely woven nests, which are delicate and light yet strong enough to protect the eggs and nestlings. Nests made by human fingers cannot compete with the complex structures created by birds, but it is fun to try, using whatever materials can be found.

**YOU WILL NEED**
A collecting bag

### MAKING A BIRD'S NEST

Show the children a photograph of a nest (such as the cup-shaped nest pictured opposite), or better still a real bird's nest, so that they can see what materials are used and how a nest might be constructed. Birds' nests are made in all sorts of shapes and sizes. A magpie's nest is an untidy assemblage of large twigs usually positioned high up among the branches, whereas the blue tit builds a neat nest of moss, wool, and feathers and often conceals it in a hole in a tree or wall. The house martin, on the other hand, molds a nest of mud against the eaves of a building.

• Encourage the children to collect suitable nesting materials. Birds use twigs, grasses, stems, rushes,

mud, moss, lichen, feathers, seedheads, sheep's wool, spiders' webs, and animal fur. Some even use man-made materials such as string, plastic twine, or bits of paper.

- Explain that nesting materials have two main functions: to provide support and to insulate.

- Remind the children how easy it is for us to collect materials, whereas a small bird makes hundreds or even thousands of journeys to gather everything it needs.

- Encourage the children to weave and thread twigs or stems together to make the base of the nest, and then line it with softer materials. The nest could be any design—large or small, open or covered—so long as it holds together.

- Most children will attempt a cup-shaped nest. A bird would weave the materials roughly in place, then sit in the center of the nest and turn around and around, pushing downward and outward with its breast to create the right shape. Encourage the children to imagine their fist is the bird's body; perhaps by turning it and applying gentle pressure they might be able to create a cup-shaped nest.

- Put the nests in trees or shrubs or in a hedge or wall. Youngsters like to believe that a bird may come along and use their nest, so encourage them to find a protected place safe from predators.

- Those who want more of a challenge could try making a nest for a particular species of bird, such as a molded mud nest for a martin or swallow. Search your local library for a children's bird book with photographs of nests to give you ideas.

# EASTER FUN

Each year some friends organize a huge Easter egg hunt in which hordes of children rampage round their garden searching for chocolate eggs hidden in all sorts of unlikely places by the elusive Easter bunny. The egg hunt is followed by eggy games —egg rolling, egg bowling, and even playing catch with raw eggs—which are all very chaotic, very messy, and great fun.

For Easter games with a bit of a difference, try combining nest making with hunting for chocolate eggs. A few years ago my children had great fun planning and organizing an Easter egg hunt for their toddler cousins. They made several little nests and hid them around the garden, filling each one with a clutch of sugar-coated chocolate eggs, as in the photograph opposite. The cousins squealed with delight when they discovered that chocolate eggs had been laid in tiny, moss-lined nests.

## DECORATIVE EASTER NEST

A large nest of twigs lined with vivid green moss or spidery grey lichen makes a festive table decoration, especially if it is filled with colored eggs. The children could decorate hard-boiled or blown chickens' eggs using paint, food coloring, tissue paper, or nail polish. The hard-boiled eggs pictured below and on page 50 were dyed by soaking them overnight in a mixture of diluted vinegar and food coloring. The children drew on the eggs with wax crayons and candles before soaking them in the coloring to produce the patterned effect.

## WOODLAND EASTER EGG HUNT

Try taking a group of young children to the woods or the park to hunt for chocolate eggs hidden by the Easter bunny.

• Before you go, have a craft session creating egg-collecting boxes.

• An adult will need to go ahead of the group to hide chocolate eggs along the chosen route.

• As the children search for eggs, encourage them to look for other things as well. Perhaps they could be asked to find egg-shaped objects, such as seeds, nuts, or pebbles, to place in their boxes alongside the chocolate eggs.

---

**YOU WILL NEED**

**DECORATIVE EASTER NEST**
- Natural materials such as moss, twigs, or lichen to make the nest
- Hard-boiled/blown chickens' eggs
- Paint/food coloring/tissue paper/nail varnish to decorate the eggs

**WOODLAND EASTER EGG HUNT**
- Chocolate eggs
- Egg-collecting boxes made by stapling a cardboard handle to the bottom half of an egg box, decorating with paints and tissue paper

## YOU WILL NEED

- Chickens' eggs
- Paper
- Chocolate eggs

## EASTER TREASURE HUNT

During one hunt for chocolate eggs, a friend's children were very disappointed to find ordinary chickens' eggs hidden in a bird's nest in the garden. But then someone noticed a bit of paper poking out of one of the eggs, so they smashed the shell to find a tightly rolled-up clue inside. This was the first clue in a treasure hunt that took them all over the garden until they eventually found a great treasure trove of chocolate eggs.

- This treasure hunt could be organized in secret—as a complete surprise for the children—or you could involve them in getting it ready.

- Help the children to blow several chickens' eggs; the empty shells will provide the hiding places for the clues. Pierce holes at both ends of the eggs, then blow the white and the yolk into a bowl (these can be used for baking). Rinse out all the blown eggs and leave them to dry.

- Write out clues on small pieces of paper. Roll up the paper as tightly as possible and insert one clue into each egg. Number the eggs as you do this so that they can be placed in the correct order for the treasure hunt.

- Hide the eggs around the garden, perhaps placing them in birds' nests made by the children (see the previous chapter).

- Let the children follow the trail, smashing the shells when they find them, until they reach the chocolate eggs.

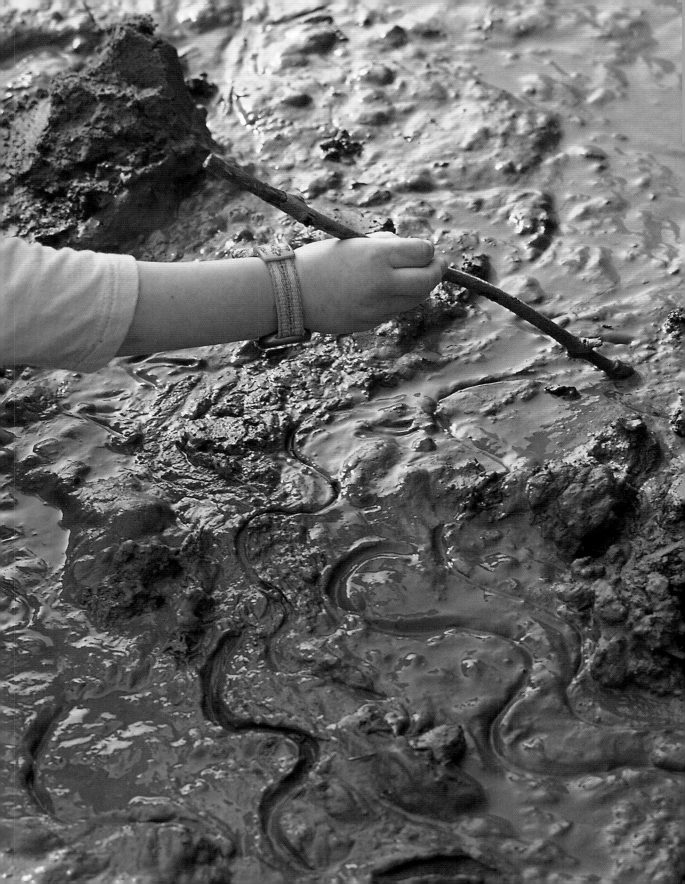

# MUD, GLORIOUS MUD!

Mud can be molded and shaped, plastered on faces, and made into pies. It squidges up between toes or dribbles pleasingly through fingers. It can even be wallowed in. This is a material that provides children with a rich range of sensations and opportunities for play. Mud is just good, clean soil, easily washed off and harmless, yet many parents shudder at the thought of their precious children becoming mudlarks. Relax. Every once in a while there is no harm in letting children wear their oldest clothes and get well and truly stuck in. It is acceptable for children to get caked in mud on the sports field, so why shouldn't they be allowed to enjoy playing with mud for its own sake, without having to worry about getting dirty?

On a wet spring walk, a friend's six-year-old daughter made a beeline for the deep, muddy puddles in a rutted path. She hesitated for a moment, glancing uncertainly at her mother, perhaps a little anxious about spoiling her immaculate pink outfit. But the temptation was just too great, and in she went, wading through every single puddle, spreading mud satisfyingly all over her pink boots, trousers, and coat, while her beaming face proclaimed "I just love mud!" A more cautious little girl was only persuaded to get muddy when told that the washing machine was fed up with washing clean clothes and longing for some real dirt. Once she got over her initial disgust, she declared, "This is amazing— I'm so muddy but I don't care!" What a wonderful sense of freedom these two girls experienced, released from the usual constraints.

A woodland walk with a friend and our four children, aged between nine and thirteen, looked set to go horribly wrong when someone slipped and fell into a patch of soft mud. But instead of the expected howls of complaint there were hoots of laughter, as mud was scooped up and daubed on faces and clothes, and suddenly a mud fight began.

Any concerns about image and fashion were abandoned, as everyone got completely plastered in gooey mud. We mothers joined in the laughter, knowing that the pleasure the children were gaining from their muddy game was far more important than worrying about dirty car seats or filthy rings around the bath. It is now several years later, and when I asked my daughter if she remembered that game she grinned and said, "Yes, it was great!"

## MUD ART

On an expedition to play tree hugging (see page 147), some of the children got stuck in the mud and had to be rescued by their giggling friends. The mud was too tempting to ignore, and squatting down by the track the children began lifting up great handfuls, letting it drip through their fingers. Before long they began molding some thicker mud into miniature mud caves and even houses with several floors. Boys and girls worked together, designing the mud dwellings, using sticks as supports, and making daub by mixing mud with grass. The trees waited for another day . . .

Here are a few suggestions for other ways in which children can make muddy works of art:

**Mud balls** On the expedition described above, the children began to roll mud to make balls. Not satisfied with this, they then coated the mud balls

with moss, leaves, bark, and even a few flowers, and piled them up to create miniature sculptures.

**Mud bowls and other sculptures** If the clay content is reasonably high, mud can be molded into all sorts of shapes that will remain intact after drying.

**Mud pies and cakes** An old favorite. Try making layers of different colors and textures, decorating with twig candles and nuts, seeds, and stones. My son tells me that his friends mold mud pies into "poo" shapes for hurling at each other. Delightful.

**Mud drawings** Use a stick for making pictures in soft mud, or dip it in thick mud for drawing on a rock or a tree trunk. Children can also make muddy hand- and footprints on rocks, paper, or—better still —each other.

**Mud cracks** Try plastering mud over a flat surface such as a stone. If the soil has a relatively high clay content a complex pattern of cracks will emerge as it dries.

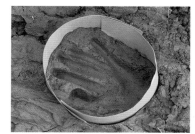  

## MAKING MUD CASTS

Walking through mud of the right consistency (not too wet and not too dry), observant children may spot the tracks of wild animals as well as human footprints. They could also make prints themselves, using their hands or bare feet, or pressing natural objects such as snail shells, leaves, twigs, or cones gently into the mud. Try using plaster of Paris to make casts of these mud prints as a record of your walk. This activity works best in clay-rich soil.

• Choose mud that is the right consistency to hold the shape of the print.

• Select existing animal or human tracks or make some new prints.

• Place the ring or square of cardboard around the print, pushing it gently in the mud to make a frame.

• Pour some water into the plastic container and carefully scatter plaster of Paris over it until the water stops soaking up the plaster. Mix with a stick. The plaster should be a thick, creamy consistency.

• Gently pour the plaster into the card frame to a depth of about 1 inch (2.5 cm).

• Leave to set for about twenty minutes, then gently pry the cast out of the ground and wrap it in newspaper to take home.

• After a couple of hours the cast will have set hard enough for you to rinse off the mud. Scrub with an old toothbrush to clean it properly. The cast can then be left as it is or perhaps the children could decorate it by painting and varnishing.

• Try this activity in a patch of soil in the garden. Soak the mud with water until it is just the right consistency and then make casts of all sorts of things, from a toy soldier to the cat's pawprint.

### YOU WILL NEED

• Strip of card about 1 foot by 2½ inches (30 cm × 6 cm), with a paperclip to fix it into a circle
• To make a square or rectangular cast, use a small cardboard box (such as a chocolate box) with the bottom removed.
• Plaster of Paris
• Water
• Plastic container
• Newspaper

### SAFETY TIPS

• Before playing with mud, cover cuts with waterproof plasters.
• Make sure hands, feet, and anywhere else exposed to mud are washed properly with soap afterward.

# CAMOUFLAGE GAMES

Using camouflage is a vital survival strategy of both predator and prey, helping either to disappear into the background. Effective camouflage is not just about color and markings, it is also about deceptive behavior patterns and a real sense of belonging to the environment. Hunter-gatherer peoples of the world try to merge with their surroundings by mimicking an animal or natural object, believing that this makes it harder for wild animals to detect their presence.

Camouflage games increase children's awareness of the environment and the ways in which wild creatures can disappear into the background. When they are looking for animals or birds, or playing games of hide-and-seek, encourage children to do the following:

• Wear muted colours with no bold outlines or logos.

• Disguise their faces. Even when the rest of the body is hidden, the shape of a face can really stand out. The children can use mud or face paints to blur the shape and change the color, or wear a cap to cast a shadow.

• Try to adopt a shape that echoes surrounding features, such as boulders or tall plants.

• Move quietly and slowly without any sudden jerks.

• Use natural features such as tree trunks, bushes, and hollows as hiding places.

• Crouch down and crawl on their stomachs so their silhouettes don't break the skyline.

• Always approach any wild animal from downwind, as most rely very heavily on their strong sense of smell.

• Keep to the shadows.

Providing camouflage may be as simple as encouraging the children to wear muted greens and

**YOU WILL NEED**
• Netting such as onion sacks or loose-meshed garden netting (for example strawberry netting) from a garden centre. Take enough lengths for each child to make a cape.
• Scissors/shears for cutting materials
• String/raffia/wool
• Face paints

**SAFETY TIP**
Supervise children using sharp shears or scissors.

browns when they are out on an expedition, or it may involve them in creating an elaborate costume. Camouflage games can be played in large gardens or parks, but they are most exciting in woodland. The games described on the following pages could be played at any time of year, but are best during late spring or early summer when the ground is drier and there is abundant vegetation.

## MAKING YOUR OWN CAMOUFLAGE

On an expedition to woodland in late spring, our children had a lot of fun making camouflage capes by weaving natural materials through lengths of garden netting. Used as a cloak or a blanket, these capes provided very effective camouflage for children lying on the woodland floor.

- Go to an area of woodland or scrub where you know you will find natural materials such as bracken, grasses, leaves, and twigs.

- Collect natural materials, then weave them through or tie them to the netting. The children may need adult help as this can be quite fiddly.

- Drape the completed capes around the children's shoulders and then paint their faces for extra effect. If the netting is long enough, cut a hole in the middle and place it right over the children's heads, like a poncho.

## BECOMING THE GREEN GIRL OR BOY

Deep in the forest, it is easy to imagine a face among the shadows, peering at us through a mask of leaves. This is the mythical Green Man, a symbol of rebirth and regeneration, whose origins and meaning remain shrouded in mystery, but whose foliate mask dates back to Roman times. Many medieval churches and cathedrals across Western Europe are decorated with sculptures of a face or mask with leaves sprouting from it. We no longer know his full story, but the Green Man could be interpreted today as a symbol of reverence for trees and nature. There is a sense that his leafy mask symbolizes something ancient and important, something both beautiful and sinister.

- Leafy headdresses and green face paint can be used with camouflage capes to create Green Girls and Boys, who gaze out at the surrounding woodland from behind their disguises. They can hide in the woods, listening and watching, trying to feel as though they are a part of nature. Allow them the space to sit quietly; if they sit for long enough perhaps animals and birds may come close to them.

## CAMOUFLAGE HIDE-AND-SEEK

The challenge in this game is to use camouflage as a means of hiding, instead of hiding behind something. Those hiding should try to blend in with the surroundings by being still and feeling comfortable with their environment. This game is most effective and exciting if played at dusk.

- Children should be dressed in muted colors or wear their camouflage capes. Face paints or mud can be used to disguise their faces.

- Choose a stretch of path for the game. Everyone should know exactly where the chosen section of path begins and ends.

- Encourage those hiding to find a place just off the path. They should hide themselves by lying, sitting, or standing in harmony with the natural shapes and contours of the place.

- The seekers then walk along the path looking for the hiders, who leap up victorious if the seekers are not able to see through their camouflage.

## CAMOUFLAGE CAPTURE

The most popular game at one countryside play group was the camouflage game. Groups of up to thirty children were split into two teams and taken to an area of open woodland and bracken. Each team had a base, and the aim was to attempt to capture the other team's base—not by force but by stealth. The children had to move slowly and carefully, using natural features for cover, trying to blend into the background and avoid being spotted. They soon learned to come to the group in green, brown, or khaki clothing, and the addition of face paint made them even harder to see.

This game can be adapted for smaller groups of children, who might play it after making their camouflage outfit. Select one child or an adult to guard a central point, which the other children have to try to creep up on and capture. The better the camouflage and the more slowly they move, the more likely they are to succeed.

## CAMOUFLAGED OBJECTS

Children always enjoy our local sculpture trail; they rush off into the woods in search of all sorts of unlikely sculptures crafted out of metal, wood, and other materials. Some sculptures are easy to spot, their harsh lines, shiny surfaces, and pale colors standing out clearly among the softer outlines and hues of the surrounding forest, but the wonderful fish tree is almost impossible to find. This rusting metallic tree with fish where there should be leaves is perfectly camouflaged, blending in seamlessly with all the natural trees surrounding it. Another favorite sculpture was a large square of carpet, its russet-colored swirls almost indistinguishable from the woodland floor.

Some objects blend with wild places, but others are easy to see. This game encourages children to search for items in places where they don't belong.

- Choose a small area in a woodland, park, or garden.

- Place a variety of man-made objects in the chosen area. Some might be easy to spot, such as a plastic cup, a saucepan, or a pink glove, but others might be harder to pick out, such as a green towel, a brown fleece, or a houseplant.

- Give the children about ten minutes to try to spot all the things that don't belong.

- Talk about the objects they discover and send them back to try again if they miss any.

- The game could be made into a competition to see who can find the most objects.

- Young children might enjoy looking for teddy bears and other cuddly toys hidden among the trees and shrubs. Make some of them easy to find and others more of a challenge.

- Make sure that all the objects are picked up after the game has finished.

# SUMMER

# MAKING THE MOST OF SUMMER

When spring moves on into summer the pace of life quickens as the natural world strives to make the most of each long, warm day. Sunshine and food are plentiful; plants take the opportunity to flower and bear fruit, animals to raise their young. Every patch of meadow and woodland, every pond, every suburban garden and urban park is buzzing with life. In even the tiniest patches of green wilderness there are different things to see each day—flowers blooming and fading, insects coming and going. This is nature's rush hour, when everything is working at full speed, taking advantage of summer's energy-giving sunshine.

For young children, the hazy days of summer stretch ahead endlessly. This is an exciting time of outdoor play, long holidays, and increased freedom. There is something different to do or see each day: search for bugs and beetles, make dens, build sculptures at the beach, or perhaps simply laze around in the sunshine, making record-breaking daisy chains or burying friends under freshly mown grass. Even summer's warm rain brings pleasures, whether it means sheltering beneath natural umbrellas of rhubarb or burdock, running barefoot through the sodden grass, or searching for snails crawling among the wet leaves.

**Early summer** In the woods the leaves of the trees are not yet fully grown, so sunshine still filters down to the forest floor; this is the season to enjoy carpets of woodland wildflowers such as bluebells. Early summer is the best time of year for getting up early, so try to rouse the children from their beds on a still morning for a picnic breakfast in the woods. Listen while the trees all around you ring with the sounds of the dawn chorus as the birds greet another bright new day.

**Mid-summer** Day length reaches its peak, yet most of the summer lies ahead. Everything is still fresh and green; this is perhaps the best time for meadows, woodland edges, and other habitats where wildflowers thrive. Each corner of uncut grassland and scrub is alive, and butterflies, bugs, grasshoppers, and crickets are just a few of the creatures to be found by those who look carefully. The summer solstice might be a time for a celebration. Try an evening walk with crêpe-paper flags and night-lights in decorated jam jars and a picnic watching the sun set over the longest day as night's wildlife begins to emerge.

**Late summer** The sun is at its hottest; many plants begin to look a little tired of the heat, and the woods are deceptively silent. Although some flowers have yet to bloom, many others are setting seed, and out in the fields it is harvest-time. Perhaps there is a family holiday to look forward to and a little more time to enjoy the natural world together, with opportunities to explore new habitats at the seaside, in a national park, or even in another country. So take your adventure bag away with you and be prepared to make lots of new discoveries.

## READY FOR SUMMER

The warmth of summer can lull us into a false sense of security. When there is no need for layers of clothes or boots, it is all too easy to set off on an expedition with no preparation at all. Yet many of summer's attractions can also be a hazard; this is when children can easily become sunburned or dehydrated or suffer from insect bites and stings. Don't get caught by surprise; plan ahead and pack the adventure bag with the following:

**Water** Take more than you think you will need. Ideally, children should each have their own bottle to drink from whenever they like. Encourage them to take small sips rather than gulping it all down at once.

**High-factor sunscreen** Apply before the expedition and take the bottle along in case further applications are needed.

**Hats** These will protect children's faces and necks from the sun.

**Suitable clothes** Children should wear T-shirts that cover their shoulders. Take additional long-sleeved shirts and perhaps long pants if out all day.

**Wet weather gear** If the weather looks changeable, pack the raingear just in case.

**Insect repellent** This is useful for deterring flies or mosquitoes. You should also include antihistamine cream for stings and insect bites.

**Supplies** Pack food that will not spoil in the heat.

# A TASTE OF EARLY SUMMER

Each May, my children watch the elder trees carefully, anxious not to miss the day when the creamy flower buds begin to burst open. They know that the honey-scented blossoms are best collected while fresh and new, before their fragrance becomes tainted with bitterness, and they long for the year's first taste of thirst-quenching elderflower cordial.

Children love to gather food for free, but harvesting from nature is more often associated with autumn berries than summer flowers. One plant that can be harvested at this time of year is the elder. This untidy shrub, usually found in hedges and along woodland edges, produces masses of cream flowerheads at the end of May and beginning of June. It has bitter-smelling leaves but its flowers are aromatic and add a subtle tang when mixed into homemade jellies and jams. Dipped into a light batter and fried, they make tasty fritters. The flowers can also be used to create a delicious, scented cordial or sorbet.

When you are gathering elderflowers, make sure you choose the freshest heads, the ones with tiny buds that have just burst open. Pick or cut the heads and place them gently into a bag or basket. Try to use them as soon as you get home.

## A RECIPE FOR ELDERFLOWER CORDIAL

- Mix the sugar and water in a large saucepan and bring to a boil, stirring until the sugar dissolves. Transfer the contents of the saucepan to a bowl.

- Grate the zest of the two lemons into the bowl. Then slice the lemons and add them to the mixture, along with the citric or tartaric acid.

- Cut most of the stalks off the elderflowers and add the flowers to the bowl.

### INGREDIENTS
- 25–30 large elderflower heads
- 4 pounds (1.8 kg) granulated sugar
- 1¾ pints (1 litre) water
- 2 lemons
- 2½ ounces (75 g) citric/tartaric acid (available from good pharmacists)

### SAFETY TIPS
- Be sure you know what you are collecting.
- Do not collect from roadside bushes, which may be polluted with exhaust fumes.

- Cover and leave to soak for 24 hours.

- Strain the mixture through muslin, squeezing out as much juice as possible.

- Pour the liquid into clean bottles.

- Store elderflower cordial in the fridge for a couple of weeks or keep frozen until required. It does not keep well at room temperature.

## USES OF ELDERFLOWER CORDIAL

Homemade elderflower cordial can be used in several different ways:

**As a refreshing drink** Dilute the cordial with still or sparkling water to create a delicious summer drink.

**To go with soft fruit** Undiluted cordial adds both sweetness and a subtle fragrance if poured over fresh strawberries or raspberries.

**As a summer sorbet** Add about 1½ pints (800 ml) of water to each 1/3 pint (200 ml) of cordial and place in a plastic container. Freeze for two to three hours, then mix well. Repeat this process three or four times to break down the ice crystals and produce a beautifully smooth, opaque sorbet. This delicately flavored sorbet is a delicious accompaniment to soft fruit and a favorite with children on a hot summer's day.

**In fruit and elderflower sauce** Simmer fruit such as plums or apricots in elderflower cordial and water until the fruit is cooked. Purée and use the sauce with vanilla ice cream.

# MEADOW MYSTERIES

A meadow is somewhere to run, long grasses tickling bare legs. It is somewhere to lie on one's back, gazing up through crisscrossed stems, searching for cloud creatures in the sky. It is somewhere to crawl and squirm, in search of hidden friends or little creatures. On memorable summer afternoons, when our families meet up in a riverside meadow, the children rush headlong into the grass, hide among the frothy Queen Anne's lace and inspect the little beetles crawling in the buttercups. They spend the whole afternoon exploring and hiding, playing and relaxing.

**WHAT YOU NEED**
- Magnifying glasses
- String
- Stick-on labels
- Bug boxes
- Old paintbrushes
- A simple field guide
- An old white sheet or tablecloth

Old hay meadows are exciting and rewarding places to explore but they are now quite rare, and meadowlike habitats can be just as much fun. Look for these along woodland edges and in woodland clearings, in churchyards and on village greens, and along footpaths and disused railway lines. Whether you are exploring a traditional meadow or a grassy clearing in a wood, treat all these habitats with respect and only visit if there is full public access. You can minimize damage by visiting meadows early in the summer, well before harvesting, or sticking to smaller patches of rough grassland.

Many of the activities described in this section involve looking for the invertebrates hiding among grasses and shrubs. Providing a child with a magnifying glass opens a door to a whole new miniature world. Don't worry about attaching names to each find; just let the children enjoy discovering where the creatures live and how they behave. For those who want to identify the invertebrates they find, there are many excellent field guides available.

## CREEPING THROUGH THE GRASS FOREST

Among the long grasses, Queen Anne's lace, and buttercups lurk hundreds of tiny creatures that children may be able to spot as they crawl slowly through a meadow. Careful investigation of frothy "cuckoo spit" left on grasses may reveal a tiny green froghopper nymph. A silken tent woven among the stems might protect baby spiders (see photo on page 70), the mother standing guard near by. Mounds of earth may turn out to be anthills, home to thousands of hardworking yellow ants. On one expedition Jo's son Dan was heard to say, "I love going through the grass like this. It looks like I'm a bug!"

- Before they start, try a little storytelling, perhaps inspired by *Alice in Wonderland* or *Honey, I Shrunk the Kids*. You could give a special sweet or drink to each of the children, telling them that it has magical shrinking powers.

- Give each child a magnifying glass and let them get right down on their hands and knees or even stomachs to creep and crawl through the long grass, encouraging them to imagine that they are part of the meadow world.

- As they crawl, get the children to look closely at the grassy forest. They might see a caterpillar munching on a leaf, a line of marching ants, or a cluster of beetles feasting on nectar in a flower.

## TINY PATHWAYS

Instead of crawling at random, the children might prefer to follow a piece of string through the grass, in the same way as botanists sometimes use a length of tape as a transect, providing a handy profile of a site. Following a string path can focus the children's attention, encouraging them to look more closely at their surroundings.

- Give each child a length of string.

- Let them choose a small area to explore and use the string to make a pathway or transect across it.

- Twigs could be used to secure the string in place.

- Encourage the children to see how many interesting things they can find along the trail.

- The trail could be laid across different habitats, perhaps moving from grass to a marshy area to the edge of a pond. Ask the children about the different types of plants and creatures they see as they crawl from one habitat to another.

## WILD PLACES UNDERFOOT

Many children have visited a variety of gardens, parks, or nature reserves and they know that each site has its own characteristics, with different wildlife habitats and places to hide and play. What they may not realize is that even very small areas have a variety of features within them. As well as using transects, scientists surveying a habitat will often record the plants found within quadrats—sample areas that are randomly situated but of a standard size and shape. Encourage the children to become scientists themselves and see what they can find within a homemade quadrat, their own little wild patch.

- Ask the children to choose a small area to explore, which they might imagine as a miniature park or nature reserve, an elf's garden, or a fairy dell.

- Give each child a couple of yards of string. Ask them to tie the ends together and enclose their special area within the string.

- Attach some stick-on labels to twigs and use these to mark out the most interesting features in each quadrat—perhaps an anthill mountain covered with a forest of grass or a piece of rotting wood that harbors a many-legged monster (otherwise known as a centipede).

- Ask the children to select features that appeal to them, whether a clump of wildflowers, a spider's nest, or a pile of rabbit droppings. Encourage them to use their imaginations—perhaps they will find a fairy's mossy bed, an elf's look-out post, or a pixie's toadstool.

- If the children decide that their wild patches are not interesting enough, they could embellish them with a few treasures from elsewhere.

- Instead of using existing features, the children could create their own miniature landscape in a corner of a garden or in a seed tray, window box, or even an eggshell. Children love to create miniature worlds that mimic reality. The tiny garden pictured at right was made in a cardboard box lined with black plastic. All sorts of little pieces of plants and other materials were collected to create the paths, flowerbeds, pond, and sitting area.

## BUSH BUGS

Meadows and other patches of uncut grassland are often surrounded by trees and shrubs, which also harbor all sorts of invertebrate insect life. This is when a sheet or tablecloth comes in handy.

- Place an old tablecloth or sheet beneath a shrub. You can put it on the ground or ask the children to hold it at each corner.

- Shake the branches of the shrub gently but firmly over the outspread cloth.

- A variety of little creatures should fall on the cloth, including small flies and beetles, ladybugs, caterpillars, and glossy, green shield bugs.

- Gently collect them in bug boxes or some other container for further investigation.

- Paintbrushes are useful for picking up the smallest creatures. Place the brush close to an insect so that it has to climb on to it.

- When the children have finished looking at the bugs and beetles, they should carefully place them back among the leaves of the shrub.

## SWEEP NETTING

On one expedition we strolled through a meadow and along a track bordered by long grasses and flowers while three little girls searched for creatures using a sweep net. It took them only a few broad strokes to catch a variety of beetles, bugs, and flies.

Sweeping a large net through long grass is the most effective way to catch the invertebrates hiding among the stems. The net should be lightweight, with a large opening, and used very gently so as not to harm anything.

- Cut the pillowcase in half horizontally, discarding the half with the opening.

- Sew a hem at least ¾ inch (2 cm) wide all the way around the cut edge, leaving a small section of hem unsewn.

- Untwist the clothes hanger and insert one end of the wire into the hem, through the unsecured section. Thread the wire all the way around inside the hem. Sew up the hem opening, leaving the ends of the wire loose inside.

## USING A SWEEP NET

- With the open edge at right angles to the ground, hold the upper rim of the net with two hands.

- Swing the net from side to side in a full arc as you walk along slowly.

- Stop sweeping after a short while and look into the net to see what you have caught. Use a bug box or magnifying glass to get a better look at your finds.

- Remember to return the creatures to the area where they were caught.

### WHAT YOU NEED
- An old pillowcase
- Sewing machine/needle and thread
- A wire clothes hanger

### SAFETY TIP
Watch out for insects that might sting.

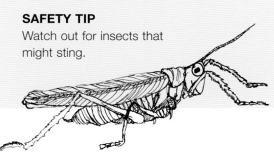

## A CLOSER LOOK AT GRASSES

If you think all grasses are the same, take another look. Children used to playing outside know that you can produce an excruciating screaming noise by blowing across some grasses, while others are sweet to suck, or have soft flowers that you can slide up the stem, or are very coarse and cut fingers.

On a family picnic, children crawling around a meadow began to collect grasses with differently shaped flowers and seedheads, searching for as many types as they could find and sticking them on a sheet of paper. As they looked increasingly carefully the game became more competitive, and they began to realize that some of the grasses that appeared at first glance to be different were in fact the same species. This is a good example of how a competition can make an activity more exciting, involving children in something that you might not have expected them to enjoy.

When children are walking or crawling in a late-summer meadow, seeds will collect in pant cuffs and shoes, or attach themselves to clothing. Try gathering them up when you get back home and sowing them in a pot to see if any will grow.

# COLORS ALL AROUND US

A group of children ranging from eighteen months to thirteen years old were each given a sticky square of cardboard (made according to the method described on page 75). They weren't very impressed until I explained their mission: to see how many tiny fragments of natural color they could fit on their cards. Then each child became completely absorbed in creating a miniature mosaic of color. Some made random arrangements and others precise patterns; some collected as many colors as possible and still others chose to look for different shades and textures of one color. They worked together, the older children helping the younger, and as they looked for colors they began to notice other things—a bee on a flower, a caterpillar on a leaf, and a whole spectrum of shades and colors, even in the grasses of the close-cropped lawn.

Most of us appreciate the rich colors of the natural world only in the context of the larger landscape, but if you look closely there is so much more to see. This is one of the simplest but also most rewarding activities. It can be enjoyed by children of all ages throughout the year, although it is particularly worthwhile during the summer months and in the autumn. Any natural or garden habitat where the children can collect little pieces of plants is suitable.

### PLAYING WITH COLOR

- Give each child a card and help them to peel the top layer off the double-sided tape.

- Ask the children to collect tiny pieces of natural color to arrange on the sticky surface.

- Tell them not to collect whole flowers and direct them toward the commonly found species.

- The children may need a little help to begin with. Show them how they might collect a section of a leaf or petal, a fluffy seed, or some grains of soil.

- Make a few suggestions if need be. Perhaps they could place red at one end of the card and green at the other, and then look for the shades of the spectrum in between. They could make a little picture out of the colors or they could focus on collecting just one type of material, such as leaves, petals, twigs, or flakes of bark. They might look for different shades and textures of one color or cover their cards in as many colors as possible.

**WHAT YOU NEED**
A handful of sticky cards, made by cutting stiff cardboard into small squares or rectangles and covering one side with a double-sided sticky tape, such as carpet tape (available from good hardware stores). Make up a few cards at a time and always keep some tucked away in the adventure bag.

**SAFETY TIP**
Direct the children away from poisonous or stinging plants.

• Try making the activity a challenge. Who can collect the most colors? Who can cover the whole surface of the card? Can anyone find all the colors of the rainbow?

• Children might stick their mosaics on white card to make greetings cards, frame them to create pictures, or cover them in sticky-backed plastic to make bookmarks.

• An alternative to making color cards is to create stained-glass windows from natural materials. Fix a sheet of sticky-backed plastic onto a cardboard frame to make the window. The children can then attach petals and leaves to the sticky plastic, trying to choose materials, such as a poppy petal or a young deciduous leaf, that will let through a little light.

• Don't be prescriptive—let the children decide what to create and how to use the colors they find.

# SUMMER SCENTS

At about the age of seven, my daughter and her friends would scour the garden for colorful fallen petals to mix and mash with water, producing their very own sweet-scented petal perfume. This favorite game was played with great absorption—though, days later, we would find the containers abandoned in a corner of the garden, full of a rotting brown mush.

The natural world is full of scents, both pleasant and unpleasant. There is the sweetness that clings to honeysuckle, rose, and elderflower, the fragrance of herbs such as mint and marjoram, the rotting-flesh odor given off by the stinkhorn fungus and hawthorn blossom, the pungency of wild garlic, the sharpness of pine resin, or the seaside tang of salt and seaweed. Summer is the best season for discovering pleasant scents—this is the time when flowering plants are working hard to attract pollinating insects.

## MAKING PERFUMED POTIONS

This fun activity can be a good game for a children's party. The children will become completely absorbed in making potions, working together to collect and mix the flowers and enjoying the sweet fragrances and the bright colors.

- Each child needs to be given a plastic cup with a little water in the bottom. Alternatively, the children could work as a team to produce one potion in a jug.

- Suggest they each find a stick for mixing.

- Ask the children to look for leaves, petals, or fruits to use in their potion. They should choose things that look nice and smell interesting.

- The children can mix their finds straight into the

### WHAT YOU NEED
- Clear plastic cups/plastic glasses/a jug
- Water
- Mortar and pestle

### SAFETY TIPS
- Remind children that potions are only for looking at and smelling—never tasting.
- Make sure they do not collect any parts of poisonous plants.

water in the container or mash them first with the mortar and pestle.

- When they have finished mixing, gather the children together and choose a name for each potion, passing them around so everyone can have a good sniff. Be warned that some bright spark usually puts something unpleasant in his or her potion!

## SECRET SMELLS

Have you ever tried to identify leaves or berries by smell alone? Some scents are so distinctive that they are unmistakable, but others we are unable to pin down until we get another clue. This activity involves trying to identify mystery natural materials from their smell.

- Seat the children and give them a blindfold each.

- Holding one of the aromatic materials at a time, let the children smell it to see if they can identify it by smell alone.

- If they are finding it difficult to identify, pass the item around so the children can feel as well as smell it.

**WHAT YOU NEED**
- Blindfolds, such as some scarves or eye-shades
- A collection of natural materials with strong scents. This might include flowers, fruits, pine needles, rotting leaves, or wild herbs such as mint, thyme, or marjoram.

# STOP AND LISTEN

Children's lives are full of noise—the television, the radio, computer games, and their own ceaseless chatter. They don't need to listen because noise surrounds them. Even when playing outside they call and shout to each other, oblivious to natural sounds. Yet it is possible for children to rest quietly, as the sleeping lions game has shown on many occasions. When a party gets too rowdy, this is an easy way to calm overexcited children and secure a few minutes' peace and quiet. The children lie down on the floor, trying to be completely still and silent. Bring in an element of competition by offering a prize for the sleepiest lion and the room will be instantly full of motionless, silent bodies lying flat on the floor.

Unless we make time to listen to them, the many sounds of the natural world pass us by. But if you listen carefully you will catch the buzzing of insects, the busy chattering of a swallow, the drumming of a woodpecker, the rustle of a breeze in the trees, the trickle of a stream, a falling leaf landing on the ground, the popping of seed cases in the sunshine . . . Try to let in the sounds of wild places.

## SLEEPING LIONS LISTENING GAME

• Invite everyone to sit or lie in a circle. Alternatively, ask them each to find their own special spot, a little apart from the other children.

• Provide the children with a challenge. Who can manage to count ten natural sounds? Who can stay quiet for the longest time? Can anyone identify any bird calls? Can anyone hear any insects or animals? The sleeping lions approach also works very well!

• Try to play this game in a wild place with few unnatural sounds, although in practice it is almost impossible to escape completely from the noise of airplanes or distant traffic.

• After a few minutes, break the silence and ask the children to describe the sounds they heard. Do they know which are natural and which are not?

• Try the game in different habitats—in a meadow, in a wood, by a stream, or in a garden.

• The most rewarding time of day for listening to sounds is either early in the morning or just as evening falls.

# WILD WEAVING

Native Americans believe that placing a web woven of natural fibers near a child's bed will trap all the bad dreams, allowing only good ones to reach the sleeper. Made from small wooden hoops crisscrossed with fibers and decorated with specially chosen feathers and other pretty, natural trinkets, dream catchers also make attractive decorations. Their origins go back a long way, to a time when Native Americans survived entirely on whatever the land could provide. Today dream catchers are widely available in many countries, but are created from man-made products such as plastic and beads as well as from natural materials. Dream catchers inspired this wild-weaving activity, in which children decorate wooden frames with a variety of natural materials.

## DECORATING THE DREAM CATCHER

- Take the dream catcher frames out on a walk and collect natural materials to weave into them.

- The children might wind a supple twig or grasses around the outer ring.

- They can also thread grasses, feathers, and flowers through the mesh.

- They might hang little trophies such as nuts, shells, or feathers from the bottom edge of the dream catcher.

- While you are out on a walk, try creating an entirely natural loom from forked sticks or bent twigs. You could then leave your wild weaving for other people to add to.

## MAKING THE FRAME

- Make each frame by bending a supple twig into a circle or an oval, securing it by wrapping yarn around the join.

- Tie a long piece of yarn (ideally the same color as the twig) on to the hoop. Pass it across to the other side and wind it around the twig a couple of times. Repeat until a web has been created.

- Attach a loop of yarn, as a handle, and fix two or three threads on the opposite side of the ring from which to hang decorations below the web.

**WHAT YOU NEED**
- Long, supple twigs
- Yarn
- Thread

# CASTLES IN THE AIR

For some children the summer is synonymous with trips to the seaside—with building sandcastles, jumping over waves, eating ice cream, and perhaps venturing on donkey rides. But a trip to the beach can be so much more than this. There may be streams to dam or divert, rockpools full of sea anemones and crabs to explore, boulders to scramble over, and sand dunes to hide among. Beach combing may reveal shells of all shapes and sizes, colored stones, jewels of sea-smoothed glass, the egg capsules, known as mermaids' purses, of the female dogfish, bleached driftwood, and perhaps the spherical shell of a sea urchin. Whether coasts are sandy, pebbly, rocky, or muddy, they offer numerous opportunities for play, discovery, and imaginary adventures.

Rivers and streams are also exciting places. On one Mediterranean holiday Hannah and Edward steadfastly refused to go to the nearby beach, preferring to return each day to their favorite spot by the river. There clear water tumbled between rocks and past shingle beaches; we swam in deep pools and slithered down little waterfalls. The children became intrepid explorers, scrambling over rocks to discover unexplored territory where scuttling lizards were fierce crocodiles, waterfalls impassable rapids, and pools shark-infested lagoons.

Castles in the air may be a little out of reach, even for the liveliest imaginations, but castle building can go far beyond upturned buckets of sand on the beach. Fortresses, palaces, dams, cairns, and miniature villages are just some of the structures that might be created on a coast or riverbank, using some imagination and plentiful supplies of rocks, pebbles, driftwood, or sand. Immersed in these activities, children may also begin to notice other things, such as the intriguing variety in the shapes and colors of stones.

## PEBBLE PLAYGROUNDS

During a visit to a wild, deserted beach my children stumbled across a half-derelict pebble village. Pebble walls surrounded the little gardens, and pebble pathways led to crumbling pebble cottages; it was as if the minute inhabitants had deserted the village in a hurry. Delighted to discover someone else's unfinished game, the children adopted the village as their own, embellishing it with more houses and towers and even gardens with seaweed trees. The time to leave came all too soon and the reluctant children were dragged away, hoping that another family might carry on where they had left off.

**Stone towers** Building at the beach can be a project for the whole family. You could have a competition to see who can build the tallest tower in the most prominent location or who can pile up the most pebbles one on top of the other. There is definitely a need for caution here: one wrong move and the whole lot might come tumbling down. You could also attempt a game of pebble skittles. Build a small stone tower and then throw smaller pebbles at it to try to knock it down. Children like throwing stones, so this game will need careful supervision.

**SAFETY TIPS**
- Children must be very well supervised when playing by a river, stream, or the sea, and should always be kept away from deep, fast-flowing water.
- Small tumbling streams are the safest watercourses for children to play in and also seem to be particularly attractive to them, probably because they are on their scale.

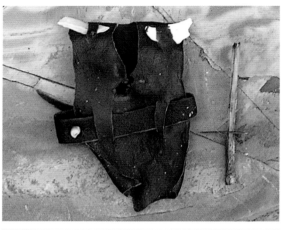

**Stones with holes** A friend's daughter was delighted and intrigued when she found a stone with a sea-eroded hole running all the way through it. She threaded the stone on a piece of twine she found and then scoured the beach for more. The result was an unusual, if rather heavy, necklace which she took home as a memento of the beach. We have followed her example but our string of stones hangs from a tree in the garden, an unusual mobile.

**Sea nymph's table and chair** The miniature dining table shown on the right was painstakingly constructed over several hours, the children patiently seeking for the tiny fragments they needed. Splinters of driftwood were turned into cutlery, fragments of seaweed became food, shells and stones became plates and bowls, and two small shells became a goblet. The feast was laid out ready to wait for the arrival of a little sea nymph or mermaid. Meanwhile another boy made equipment for a miniature sea warrior; the photograph above left shows the tiny kelp armor with its shell pins and epaulettes, and beside it a tiny sword.

**Pebble fortresses** This elaborate fortress was made using pebbles of all shapes and sizes, along with driftwood and rope found washed up on the beach.

**Stone cairns** Try building conical cairns along the shore just as the tide is on the turn. Whose cairn will withstand the incoming sea the longest?

**Pebble patterns and pictures** Collect pebbles of different sizes and colors, and use them to make collages on the beach or a nearby rock.

**Pebble treasure** Those with very sharp eyes might be lucky enough to find fossils or semiprecious stones.

**SAFETY TIP**
Young children playing with stones and pebbles should be closely supervised at all times.

## SAND STRUCTURES

**Dribble castles** Handfuls of wet sand from below the high-tide mark drip pleasingly between the fingers to produce wonderfully gothic dribble castles. The sand must be exactly the right consistency: wet enough to drip through the fingers yet firm enough to stay in place. Try bringing in an element of competition. Who can build the tallest dribble tower? How many castles can the children make?

**Sand sculptures** Walking along a huge beach, we came across an elegant, curvaceous mermaid staring up at us from the sand. She was perfectly molded, down to the detail of the hairs on her head and the scales on her tail. Inspired, the children immediately rushed off to make their own sand sculptures. After much careful shaping, a turtle and a dolphin emerged from the surface of the beach.

**Shell mosaics** During one holiday our children found hundreds of shells littering a remote beach. Instead of collecting them in their buckets, they decided to make shell pictures, producing carefully designed mosaics of a crab and a dolphin which they left on the beach for others to find. Children may find it hard to leave their masterpieces behind —so try to record them with a camera; perhaps you could build up an album of ephemeral art works made in different places.

**Shell collections** Children love to collect shells of different shapes and sizes. If you already have a collection of shells at home, perhaps the children could use them to make mosaics in a sandpit or flowerbed. For a more permanent design, try setting the shells into plaster of Paris.

## FLOTSAM AND JETSAM SCULPTURES

Many beaches are littered with non-biodegradable waste, most of which comes from ships out at sea. This trash is unsightly, but some of it might be used for creating unusual sculptures, and in the process of collecting materials you will be helping to clear up the mess on the beach. Imagine your surprise if, after you clambered down a long, narrow cliff path to a deserted beach, you discovered a life-size flotsam and jetsam horse with a pink flip-flop tongue and a thick coat of knotted ropes! This is exactly what happened to Jo and her children; although disappointed to find so much garbage on the beach, they were completely enchanted by the crazy horse. The rest of the holiday was spent beach combing and constructing all manner of weird and wonderful creatures from bits and pieces of plastic and rope. Their favorite was a lion with an orange rope mane and rubber glove feet, which they left behind to guard the narrow entrance to a secret beach in the hope that it would surprise and inspire another family.

**SAFETY TIPS**
- Adult supervision is required at all times on a beach.
- Check that the rubbish is not contaminated with oil or tar and is safe to play with.
- Do not collect plastic containers that may have been used for storing toxic materials.
- All unused beach rubbish should be left in a neat pile once the sculpture is complete—make this an opportunity to help clean up the beach.

# CORN DOLLIES

It is thought that straw from the harvest has been woven or plaited into corn dollies ever since people began to grow grain. The name "dolly" is somewhat misleading. Corn dollies were traditionally knots, fans, lanterns, and all sorts of other shapes, but only rarely did they resemble dolls. They originally had great ritual significance; it was believed that they were the very embodiment of the crop's spirit and could help to ensure the success of the next year's harvest. They were often used to decorate the table during the end-of-harvest feast, before being hung in the farm kitchen until the next year's harvest-time. Leftover straw is still used for making corn dollies, but nowadays they are for decorative rather than ritual purposes.

On an expedition to a harvested cornfield, a gang of children gathered cut straw and some of the finer grasses growing along the field margin. They began twisting and plaiting the stems to make a motley collection of corn dollies and corn creatures, of which they were very proud! Later they built dens in the long, cut grass and ran through the stubble, making the most of those last few golden hours of freedom at the end of the long summer holiday. Some of the corn and grasses were also taken home to make the corn man illustrated above.

## MAKING A CORN DOLLY

- Tie a bunch of stems together into a neat bundle using raffia, and trim the ends with the scissors or shears.

- Divide the straw of the lower half into two sections to make the legs and feet of the corn dolly, then tie them with raffia.

- Using raffia, attach a thinner bundle of straw at right angles to the dolly to form the arms.

- Weave in finer grasses, leaves, or seeds to make details as you wish.

### WHAT YOU NEED
- Straw and some leftover ears of wheat or barley collected from a harvested field
- Some finer grasses and a few leaves and seeds
- Raffia
- Scissors/shears

### SAFETY TIP
Supervise young children working with sharp shears or scissors.

# AUTUMN

# MAKING THE MOST OF AUTUMN

Autumn creeps upon us almost imperceptibly; as the heat of summer gradually fades away, the evenings become cooler, and little by little the days get shorter. A softer, subtler light replaces summer's harsh sunshine, and on misty mornings heavy dew coats the grass or scatters like pearl drops among strings of cobwebs. The growing season has ended and with the first hint of frost the leaves begin to change color in preparation for falling. Children may notice some of these changes: they feel a chill in the air, they no longer have to go to sleep while it's still light, they can play in the crisp, colored leaves, raid chestnut trees, and hunt for juicy berries.

Autumn is the season of nature's harvest, with more wild food available than at any other time of year. Animals and birds feast and gather stores of the ripening fruits and seeds, inadvertently helping to spread plants to new places. Creatures of every kind prepare for the winter—some build up their strength for migration to warmer countries, while others put on body fat to help them survive the cold months ahead. In the human world, the cereal harvest has already been gathered in, but now is the time for orchard fruits, for nuts and berries.

When our lives were inextricably linked to the year's seasons, autumn was the time for preserving and storing food to make it last over the winter. But this connection with the year's cycle has become distant now that so many people in the developed world eat whatever they like, whenever they like. Supermarket shelves are piled high with goodies from all over the globe and we can eat strawberries all year round, if we so wish. Children need to reconnect with the natural world and its seasons if they are to appreciate how their lives depend on the growth and production of food.

There is something deeply satisfying about gathering food for free; memories of childhood autumns are often full of purple-stained fingers and the sweet taste of berries. Blackberries grow at just the right height for small children to graze them straight from the bush. Choose bramble bushes away from roads and let the children enjoy a natural feast, but try to persuade them to save a few to take home. Even if they are not keen on blackberry pie, they will be unable to resist smoothies made from a handful of frozen blackberries blended with natural yogurt and a little honey. Berries are the only wild crop still foraged by significant numbers of people and therefore play a special role in linking us to the countryside. Take the children out to collect nature's harvest—berries, sweet chestnuts in their spiky shells, crab apples, wild damsons and sloes—and reinforce the connection between our lives and the earth's natural rhythms.

# NATURAL PAINTING

During an autumn walk, children from a preschool noticed a heavy crop of purple elderberries hanging down over the path and insisted on taking some away with them. Back at the school they grabbed handfuls of the berries and squeezed until the deep red juice dripped between their fingers. This became their very own blood-colored "paint," which they used enthusiastically to create handprints and pictures as reminders of their autumn walk.

The natural world has long been a source of pigments for dyes. Although the proper extraction and fixing of dyes is a complex technical process, children can have a lot of fun experimenting and getting messy as they discover that different plant materials produce different colors. Several wild fruits and leaves make color quite readily: purple can be squeezed out of elderberries and blackberries, yellow from crab apples, a deep blue-black from sloes and damsons, and subtle shades of green from grass.

Ancient Aboriginal rock paintings of animals and mysterious holy spirits, seen by the children on an Australian holiday, provided inspiration for one expedition along the edge of a wood to discover natural sources of color. The aim was to make our own paints and to use them to create patterns and pictures on tree trunks and pieces of bark. There was an element of surprise involved, as the children couldn't always predict the colors that their raw materials would produce.

## MAKING PAINTS

- Encourage the children to look around and predict which plant materials might produce colors. On this expedition, the children decided to experiment with elderberries, blackberries, grass, and rose hips.

- If you are not confident about avoiding poisonous berries, take a clearly illustrated field guide with you or go out with someone who is able to identify wild plants.

- Place one material at a time in the mortar and mash it with the pestle, adding water if necessary. Some children enjoy getting completely stuck into this activity, mixing with their bare hands and smearing color up their arms and on their faces like war paint.

- Ask the children whether they have produced the color they predicted. Some colors are strong and vibrant, others are subtler and will be harder to extract.

- For a smooth paint, pass the mixture through a tea strainer into a container.

- Use the paint to decorate large leaves, pieces of bark, or a tree trunk. Try creating pictures, patterns, or handprints, or paint arrows to make a trail that others can follow.

- The more subtle colors are not easy to use effectively outside. Take them home in the lidded containers so that the children can use them on paper, painting a picture or printing a pattern as a reminder of autumn's natural pigments.

### WHAT YOU NEED
- Mortar and pestle
- Small plastic bowls and lidded containers such as film containers
- Water
- Tea strainer
- Paper and old paintbrushes
- Old clothes (some of the colors will stain)

### SAFETY TIPS
- Only make dyes using berries from non-poisonous plants.
- If you are unsure about plant identification, take a field guide with you.
- Make sure the children wash their hands thoroughly when they've finished.

# AUTUMN COLLECTIONS

Early natural historians gathered much of their knowledge about the countryside by making collections. They stole eggs from birds' nests, pressed wildflowers, and preserved insects, making detailed notes about their finds and piecing together a picture of ecological diversity. Such collections are now frowned upon, but autumn's overwhelming abundance of colored leaves, fruits, and seeds still allows us to gather natural souvenirs.

Children love to make collections, whether they are of game cards, football medals, or stickers or the more traditional marbles or conkers. Collections are lovingly counted, sorted, compared—and simply enjoyed for their own sake. In autumn children besiege every accessible horse chestnut tree, eager to find the biggest, fattest, shiniest, most perfect conker. They pry open each spiky, dark green case to reveal a smooth, glossy chestnut nestling in its soft white bed, and weigh down their pockets with the biggest and best specimens. Ostensibly gathered for conker fights, most of the collections are just squirrelled away in boxes or tins, to be brought out now and again for counting, arranging, and comparing. Perhaps the game of conkers is itself only an excuse for the sheer enjoyment of making and keeping a collection.

## SEED-COLLECTING

Although most trees produce vast numbers of seeds, only a very few will find a suitable place to germinate and grow, and the majority will be eaten or simply rot away. This means that there will be plenty of seeds available for children to collect and put to a creative use.

**Maple seeds** Throw the "helicopter" seeds of the maple family in the air to see how well they spin back down to earth.

**Acorns** There is something very pleasing about prying acorns gently out of their cups. Leave the acorns as squirrel food, but keep the cups for use in imaginary games, perhaps to make a little tea set for an elf house.

**Hazelnuts** These can be gathered from the hedges and are delicious to eat when ripe.

**Rose hips** Gather ruby-red rose hips to make syrup; a cup of rose-hip pulp yields more vitamin C than forty oranges. However, children are much more impressed by the seeds, which are covered in tickly hairs and make an effective itching powder when removed from the hips! Keep a few rose hips and other berries somewhere cool until December as they will come in handy for making the natural decorations described on page 131.

**Cones** These can be used for a variety of craft activities. On one autumn walk, a group of boys collected pine cones and, attaching twigs as legs, made them into pine pigs, which they lined up along a branch. The addition of bracken wings might have made the pigs fly . . . Try collecting different types of cone to see how many different animals can be created entirely from natural materials, perhaps using twigs for legs, seeds for eyes, and leaves for ears.

**SAFETY TIP**
Make sure the children do not collect any poisonous materials.

## GROWING TREES

After a lengthy autumnal ramble along woodland tracks, the children emptied their pockets to reveal a collection of smooth, shiny acorns. They buried some in plant pots, which they left out in the garden and promptly forgot all about. The following spring they rediscovered the pots and noticed small green shoots pushing their way upward in search of light. During that summer, the children watered the tiny seedlings carefully, watching as they grew stronger. The following winter they planted them out on the village green, where the young plants would have space to grow.

Tree seeds need a period of cold before they will germinate, so growing them is a relatively easy but rather long-term project. The young trees can be kept in a pot for a couple of years, but should then be planted out in an appropriate place (contact a local nature conservation organization for advice). This is a practical way to involve children in creating habitats for the future, but it is important that trees are planted in a suitable location and that someone is responsible for their after-care.

# FOREST MOBILES

Combining the pleasure and excitement of collecting with the creation of an autumnal keepsake, this activity will continue to remind the children of autumn once winter has arrived.

### MAKING A MOBILE

- While out on an autumn expedition, collect treasures such as leaves, chestnuts, acorns, pinecones, winged maple seeds, beech mast, and bark from the forest floor. Look for rose hips and other berries along a hedge or for grasses and seedheads in a meadow.

- Let the children choose their own treasures—the things they think are special and beautiful—but make sure they only collect plentiful items.

- Either take the collection home or make the mobile during the expedition.

- Choose a stick about 1 foot (30 cm) long. If you wish to make a more complex mobile, select some shorter ones too.

- Make holes through the seeds and nuts using a skewer or bradawl (this may need to be done by an adult).

- Tie a knot at one end of each length of string or wool, then use the tapestry needle to thread the treasures on the strings. Try to thread a mixture of heavy and light items on each string so the weight is evenly distributed.

- Experiment with shape, size, and color, trying out different arrangements of seeds and leaves for the best effect.

- Tie the strings to the stick, balancing them carefully along its length. Alternatively, make a more complex mobile with extra layers of horizontal sticks. Then attach one long piece of wool or string to both ends of the top stick to make a handle.

- Hang the mobile among the trees to enjoy on future walks, or take it home and put it outside a window where you can watch it blow in the wind, changing slowly as autumn moves on into winter.

**WHAT YOU NEED**
- Collecting bag
- String/wool
- Skewer/bradawl
- Scissors
- Tapestry needles

**SAFETY TIPS**
- Ensure that children do not collect poisonous materials.
- Adult supervision is required when children are using a skewer, bradawl or tapestry needle.

# MAGIC CARPETS

The magic carpets of children's storybooks take you on a roller coaster ride to anywhere. Perhaps they are tightly woven and richly patterned with exotic and intricate designs in warm autumnal colors—but then again maybe details like these can only be filled in by each person's own imagination . . .

During a visit to an arboretum vibrant with autumn color, we found a large, neat rectangle of sticks on the grass—an empty frame waiting to be filled, perhaps. A little further on we met a party of schoolchildren eagerly collecting leaves, fir cones, conkers, pine needles, and seeds from the woodland floor. Returning to the frame of sticks we found children filling it with careful collages of their finds. They each worked on their own section, some making patterns and shapes, others creating pictures of animals; they all had their own way of working with the particular materials they had chosen. We discovered several more giant collages carpeting the ground, all beautifully constructed and left for others to discover. There were teddy bear shapes made from conkers and cones, circles of bright leaves decorated with berries, grass shaped into nests, and what seemed to be simply random patterns of autumn color. Made entirely from natural materials found in the arboretum, these ephemeral pieces of art showed imaginative use of shape, texture, and color. We found out later that they were meant to be magic carpets, created as part of an autumnal art project for local schools called TreeScape.

### SAFETY TIP
Make sure that children do not collect any poisonous materials.

## MAKING A MAGIC CARPET

Children with lively imaginations might dream of flying off to who knows where on a magic carpet created with their own treasured collection of leaves and seeds. This is an ideal family project, appealing to all ages. It is a great way of using locally found materials to capture feelings about a place at a particular moment, and it will bring pleasure and even inspiration to other people.

Magic carpets can be made on any scale, and the children should take their inspiration from the materials themselves. One child used red berries to make a face staring up from the grass, while another created a beautifully framed and intricately designed pattern.

During an expedition involving a large group of children, the boys and girls split forces to work out their own interpretations of a magic carpet. The girls created an imaginative fish from bark and colorful leaves; the boys made a detailed picture inspired by their surroundings, featuring a fire, a tree, and a peacock. Both groups found their own ways of using the natural materials, working together as a team.

Like all ephemeral art, magic carpets can be revisited to see how they change with the effects of time, nature, and the elements, as the inevitable process of decay sets in.

# ELF HOUSES

Wild creatures are generally elusive, hard for watchful adults to spot let alone groups of boisterous children. Much as we might know about badgers and foxes, weasels and deer, we very rarely see these creatures, and we may even question whether they are out there at all. It is quite understandable, therefore, when children believe that tiny people—secretive fairies or brave elves—live in woods and gardens, silently watching us and always avoiding us, just as animals do.

Building elf houses from whatever materials can be found is a great outlet for lively imaginations in almost any environment. Jake and Edward even made them in a corner of the school playground, using only soil, a few stones and twigs, and liberal quantities of imagination. Girls and boys of all ages love to create their own little worlds, playing with such deep intensity that nothing can break into the vivid, magical places they imagine.

## MAKING ELF HOUSES

Elf houses can be built anywhere, provided there are a few natural materials to use such as the fallen leaves, fruits, and nuts that are plentiful in autumn. Don't take anything with you—this activity is all about making the most of whatever is available and working out how different objects might be used.

Perhaps these elves and fairies are waiting for the children to build them houses to move into once they have the woods to themselves again. The little people of the forest may like to live in a dark hole near the base of a tree, with a soft mossy bed and a store of hazelnuts for food. Or they might prefer a hollow in the ground beneath a roof of twigs and leaves, with a stone table set with acorn cups and a feast of hawthorn berries on a leaf plate. An elfin knight may need a lookout post, such as a niche in a tree trunk, accessible only by a tiny ladder and defended with a tough bark door.

• Find an appropriate spot to build an elf house, perhaps between the roots of a tree, in a hollow stump, among a pile of stones, or in a dip in the ground. The children need to choose their own place, somewhere that captures their imagination and has all the elements they feel are important.

• Search for bracken, twigs, moss, hazelnuts, beech mast, cones, acorns, or whatever other suitable

items can be found. As the children search and play they will become more familiar with natural materials, and perhaps begin to develop an awareness of the never-ending processes of growth and decay as they find rotting leaves or chewed nuts.

- Allow the children plenty of time to create whatever they want to create.

- Choose somewhere that you will be able to return to easily. If the elf houses are accessible, but in a place that will not be disturbed, they might provide the start of an ongoing game, in which the children build and adapt a castle compound or miniature village.

- On one expedition, an inventive boy made miniature bows and arrows from twigs. Although only a few inches long, they really worked and were quite good enough to arm woodland elves. There was even a tiny quiver, made out of a hollow stem.

- Try visiting different natural environments so that children can experiment with a variety of materials.

- Perhaps a corner of the garden could be devoted to versions of the elf-house game. The children might make holiday cottages for the dollhouse dolls, a fortified castle for a battalion of toy soldiers, or stables and barns for plastic farm animals. Here is a chance to extend boundaries by taking an indoor game outdoors, creating many more opportunities for imaginative play than manufactured toys can offer.

**SAFETY TIPS**
- Do not let children collect fungi or poisonous berries.
- Make sure they wash their hands thoroughly after building elf houses.

# SPYING ON THE TREETOPS

We may notice the things around us at ground or eye level, but we rarely look up to see what is going on above us. On a woodland walk the habitat of the tree canopy might go completely unnoticed, yet it is a complex world of intertwining branches and leaves inhabited by birds, squirrels, and a whole host of invertebrates.

Perhaps the best way to look up into the canopy is to lie down, somewhere you can gaze into the treetops. But there is also another method: use a mirror to gain a clear view of the treetop world as you walk around the wood.

At our local sculpture trail several old car wing mirrors have been placed high up among a circle of trees. A favorite game was to see who could spot the most mirrors—pretty tricky as each one was camouflaged by its reflection of the surrounding canopy.

## HOW TO SPY ON THE TREETOPS

• Show the children how to hold a mirror across the bridge of their nose, just below the eyes. Looking down into a mirror held in this way gives a perfect view of everything above.

• Encourage the children to keep the mirror in this position and walk around slowly, looking at the shapes of the branches and the colors of the leaves and watching out for birds and squirrels.

• Ask the children to hold the mirror in different positions to see the world in different ways.

• Place a few mirrors separately on the woodland floor and encourage the children to spot them. Alternatively, put several mirrors together on the ground so the children can look into a magical mirror pool reflecting the trees and the sky.

• The varied color of leaves in autumn makes this season the ideal time to explore the canopy, but the activity can be enjoyed at any time of year.

**WHAT YOU NEED**

Small mirrors, such as make-up mirrors, or the larger and less breakable mirrored tiles.

**SAFETY TIPS**

• Encourage the children to walk slowly to avoid tripping over.
• Check there are no roots or other obstacles in the way.
• Remind the children to use mirrors very carefully. Take the mirrors away from them as soon as they have finished the activity.

# LOADS OF LEAVES

Rumor has it there is a wish for anyone who catches a leaf as it floats down from a branch, twisting and turning in the breeze. Having captured sunlight all summer, in autumn the leaves of deciduous trees lose their greenness as they begin to age and die before falling to the ground. This is a wonderful time to walk in the woods, kicking the crisp leaves or using them for wild games and other leafy activities.

## SPECIAL LEAVES

Children enjoy searching for special leaves, whether scouring a lawn for the elusive four-leafed clover, hunting down the biggest leaf they can find, perhaps to use as a makeshift umbrella, or collecting the brightest leaves of autumn. But if they were to pick out just one or two leaves from the millions in a wood, would they be able to identify their distinctive characteristics?

When they were asked to select two special leaves, the three girls pictured above chose in very different ways. One picked a yellow and a red leaf because she was attracted by the bright colors, and another chose two maple leaves because she liked their prominent red veins. The third child was intrigued by the lumps she noticed on a brown oak leaf. When told that they were spangle galls (growths induced by the presence of a wasp grub) she chose two more of the same leaves, because she didn't want the tiny grubs to be trodden on and squashed. Each child had her own reasons for her choice, and when the leaves were mixed up with many others each had no difficulty in finding her own again.

- Encourage the children to look for just two leaves that they particularly like.

- When they have all chosen two special leaves, gather the children together and ask everyone to explain why they chose their particular leaves and what they like about them.

- Look closely at the leaves, comparing and contrasting their shapes and colors. Have any been nibbled and if so what might have been eating them? Do any have creatures living on or inside them?

- Encourage the children to examine every detail of each leaf.

- Collect all the leaves into a bag or onto a coat and mix them up. Then spread them out on the ground and see if everyone can recognize his or her own leaves.

## LURKING IN THE LEAVES

Lying on the woodland floor and observing the trees from a new angle, children can feel that they have become a part of the forest.

• Encourage them each to find their own space to lie down in, then cover their bodies with fallen leaves so they appear to blend into the forest floor, rather like the mythical Green Man with his ability to melt into the trees.

• Place a few leaves gently over their faces and allow them a few minutes to lie there, part of the forest floor, surrounded by the sweet, musty scent of autumn.

• You could pre-arrange a signal to make them all jump up when you think they have spent long enough lurking in the leaves. Or perhaps this could be a game of hide-and-seek—can the seekers spot their friends among the leaves?

## PLAYING LEAF PILES

Central to a friend's childhood memories of fall in New York State is the recollection of creating huge leaf piles, with everyone working together to rake up the crisp, dry leaves. She remembers the anticipation she felt as she lay on the soft mound waiting to be buried in more armfuls of leaves, and the sweet earthy scents and crackling sounds of her autumn blanket. This is a wild and boisterous game, with children rushing all at once into the heap, an excited mass of bodies becoming completely submerged as they throw leaves up in the air and at each other.

• Rake and carry leaves to make a big pile. Restrain the children from playing in it right away—the bigger the pile, the more fun the game.

• Use the rug or groundsheet to transport leaves to the heap more efficiently.

**WHAT YOU NEED**
- A couple of rakes
- A travelling rug/groundsheet
- Dry weather! This activity only works when the leaves are dry and crisp—wet, mushy leaves would not have quite the same appeal.

**SAFETY TIPS**
- This game is fun, exciting, and wild—and will need careful supervision, especially if some of the children are very small.
- Children using rakes should be particularly well supervised.

• When the pile is ready, let the children rush into it and then hurl armfuls of leaves at each other.

• Alternatively, let the children take it in turns to lie down on the mound and have a rug full of leaves emptied over them. They can lie for a while under their autumn blanket before bursting out again.

# WOODLAND MONSTERS

Lurking in the woods there may be all sorts of magical monsters just longing to be discovered and recognized for what they really are. Hiding in an old, gnarled tree stump or submerged in a craggy rock face, a whole horde of weird and wonderful creatures may lie out there, waiting to be released by an observant child.

During a visit to a forest we discovered a man (pictured bottom right), made from cut wood. He stood there guarding the path, watching all those who came and went. We wondered who had made him or whether a wicked witch had turned some hapless visitor to wood . . .

### SEARCHING FOR MONSTERS

This game lends itself to storytelling and make-believe; perhaps you could start with a story along the following lines:

*A long, long time ago, a group of monsters lived deep in the heart of these woods. Although they looked pretty scary, they weren't bad monsters, but lived out their lives peacefully among the trees, grazing on nuts and looking after the forest and all who lived there. But one day a wicked old witch came along, a greedy, selfish witch who decided that she liked these woods so much she wanted them all for herself. The wicked witch ignored the monsters' pleas and cast a spell that made them merge into the rocks, trees, and earth of the woodland. It seemed that they were destined to stay hidden there forever. The witch moved on to other places, forgetting all about this wonderful wood and its captive monsters. But perhaps you can help them, for rumor has it that sharp-eyed children can free the friendly monsters, just by finding them and recognizing them for what they really are . . .*

**SAFETY TIP**
Keep the children together in a supervised group when exploring a wood, coast, or other wild environment.

• Encourage the children to search for monsters. If they look at tree stumps, exposed roots, or gnarled trunks they may see something that resembles an eye or a mouth, a horn or a claw.

• By adding some grass or moss, nuts or twigs, the children can reveal the magical creatures. They may like to each make their own monsters or they could work together to create one big monster, perhaps from a fallen tree trunk.

• Once revealed, the monsters can be left for others to find, and perhaps be played with and improved on future expeditions.

• This game may be played at other times of year and in many different environments. Try it in a more open, rocky setting or even at the coast, where monsters might be found lurking in boulders or under the sand.

# COLORFUL CROWNS

We celebrated autumn's colors at a local arboretum, making crowns and hats from a wonderful variety of fallen leaves and seeds. Children from four to fifteen years old joined this hat-making party, scouring the ground for colorful berries and leaves, as well as pinecones, chestnuts, and anything else they could find. In a woodland clearing the children worked together to create a startling array of headgear. They were joined by another family, out to enjoy the autumn colors, whose two young children loved making a memento of their walk.

### WHAT YOU NEED

- Thin cardboard (such as cereal boxes) cut into strips about 2–2½ inches by 20 inches (5–6 cm × 50 cm) with double-sided sticky tape attached along one side of each strip.
- Stapler
- Extra double-sided sticky tape
- Hole punch

### SAFETY TIPS

- Ensure that children collecting natural materials do not pick poisonous berries or cause damage to plants.
- Adult supervision is required when children are using needles or staplers.
- Keep candles away from foliage.

### MAKING THE CROWNS

- Collect natural materials such as leaves, pine needles, and seeds.

- Provide each child with a strip of prepared card and peel off the outer layer of double-sided tape to expose the sticky surface beneath.

- Encourage the children to choose anything they like from the collected materials to stick to their card strip.

- Use the stapler or some more tape for anything that doesn't stick to the strip easily. The punch can be used to make holes through which stems can be threaded.

- Try this activity in parkland, woodland, or a garden where there is a reasonable selection of different leaves and seeds. This is an ideal game for an outdoor birthday party (see "Outdoor Parties," page 164).

### CREATING OTHER COSTUMES

**Necklaces and bracelets** Try making these by threading specially chosen colored leaves and seeds on wool or raffia, using a tapestry needle.

**Brooches** These can be made with smaller pieces of cardboard. Stick a colorful leaf to the double-sided tape and then staple leaves in contrasting colors on top. Attach a safety pin to the back of the cardboard with a narrow piece of tape.

**Masks** Decorate cardboard templates with colorful leaves to make festive masks.

**Cloaks** Try making a seasonal cloak by threading leaves through the mesh of a piece of garden net or attaching them to an old piece of fabric. (For further details see the instructions for making a camouflage cape on pages 56–58.)

# WINTER

# MAKING THE MOST OF WINTER

Freezing mornings, interminable grey skies, fog and bitter winds—no wonder the comforting warmth of home tempts so many of us to stay indoors during the dark months of winter. Yet this season of hibernation and dormancy is an exhilarating time to venture outside, and some of the most memorable outdoor experiences await you in winter's wonderland.

There is so much to see and enjoy in winter. Young children love to scrunch through the frost, blowing dragon smoke into the chilly air, or march in the rain wrapped from head to foot in their rain gear. Older children might enjoy leaning into the force of a strong wind, running from the pounding waves on an empty beach, or scrambling up into leafless trees to spy on the grown-ups. Quieter, more watchful observers may be able to find overwintering flocks of birds, follow animal tracks through the snow, or spot last autumn's seedheads outlined in frost. A winter walk can be a time of great companionship as well as an opportunity to witness the process of change as the year creeps toward spring. Don't stay cooped up indoors—wrap up warm and get outside, ready to take whatever the elements might hurl at you.

Winter is both an end and a beginning, for in this death of the year sharp-eyed children may find all sorts of signs and clues to show them that nature is waiting patiently to burst into life at the first hint of spring. In winter, day is dwarfed by night, and all living things must find a way to beat the cold and dark and survive. Deciduous trees and shrubs shed their leaves while many smaller plants die back completely, keeping snug deep in the soil as roots or bulbs, or overwintering as seeds inside a tough protective coating. The waxy leaves and needles of evergreen plants are able to withstand the ravages of winter, and a few plants even seem to thrive on winter's cold and damp, such as the vibrant green mosses that coat rotten logs.

Many wild creatures survive the winter by reducing their level of activity. Some simply slow their metabolism a little, resting during the coldest days and nights. A few species enter full hibernation, a drastic survival mechanism which causes body temperature to plummet so low that life only just continues to tick over. Hibernating animals should never be disturbed. Their ability to last through the winter depends on whether they have built up

sufficient fat reserves, and emerging from their torpid state uses up valuable energy. Most insects overwinter in egg or chrysalis form, but some manage to survive as adults; butterflies found in the house should be left in peace until the spring arrives. Ladybugs, lacewings, and spiders shelter inside hollow stems or cracks in tree bark.

Birds have a variety of survival strategies. By winter, most insectivorous species have long since flown to tropical countries, where the constant warmth ensures a plentiful supply of insects all year round. Those birds that stay put have to search much harder for their food. Some species, however, may migrate to our temperate regions from the frozen tundra, choosing to overwinter in a place where they can at least find berries on the trees or grubs and worms in the soil. Try visiting coastal wetlands to see hundreds of overwintering shorebirds and ducks feeding on mud- and sandflats, or look for wild geese grazing on open fields.

## READY FOR WINTER

There is no such thing as bad weather, only the wrong clothes. It is particularly important to be well prepared for winter expeditions, as cold and wet children quickly become disheartened. But if they are well wrapped up, even very young children will enjoy the thrill of winter.

**Footwear** Children should wear either snow boots or sturdy walking boots. Two pairs of well-fitting socks should be worn for extra warmth. If there is snow, make sure footwear fits snugly so that the snow can't get inside them.

**Warm clothes** Several thinner layers are warmer than one thick one and enable children running about to shed an outer layer without the risk of catching a chill. Tights worn under trousers are a good idea, as is a vest and long-sleeved shirt beneath a fleece and coat.

**Waterproof outerwear** Come wind, rain, or snow, a decent set of waterproof outerwear will protect children from whatever the elements have in store.

**Gloves/mittens** Small children get miserable very quickly if their hands are too cold, yet given the chance they will want to play with ice and snow. Gloves should be warm and waterproof. Take along a couple of extra pairs, just in case.

**Hats** Children should always wear a hat in cold weather, ideally a ski mask or a hat with cozy flaps.

**Supplies** Even on a short outing some supplies will provide a useful diversion. Pack the adventure bag with something warming, perhaps a flask of soup or baked potatoes wrapped in foil, and include some chocolate and dried fruit.

# ICY ADVENTURES

Children feel cheated if winter slips by without at least one snowfall and several icy days when all the puddles freeze and each blade of grass is coated with frost. Winter walks on freezing days are most rewarding along rutted tracks, where children will want to slide or jump on the frozen puddles, then pick up the pieces of ice and smash them into hundreds of glittering fragments. Although the deep water of frozen ponds or rivers must always be avoided, puddles on tracks or fields can provide safe sheets of ice to enjoy under adult supervision.

Outings with very small children into the ice and snow should be kept quite short. Let them enjoy a quick burst of winter before retreating back into the warmth.

### PLAYING ICE GAMES

Frozen floodwater in a field provides a natural ice rink, somewhere to slide and enjoy hours of fun. Here are some suggestions for games on ice:

**Ice hockey** Find some long sticks and a pebble or piece of ice to make do as the puck, and you have a DIY ice hockey game.

**Curling** Play your own version of curling by sliding chunks of ice, or better still smooth pebbles, across a natural ice rink. Whose pebble will slide the furthest?

**Ice skittles** Slide pieces of ice across the rink to knock down a target such as a stick or a carefully balanced heap of stones.

**Ice windows** A thin sheet of ice makes a natural window through which the wintry world can be viewed. Children can see who can pick up the largest sheet of ice without breaking it, or try standing a huge sheet on its side to create a very big window. On one wintry walk we arranged several ice windows in the branches of a tree, creating a dramatic sculpture. We wondered

whether it would still be there if we returned the next day, but there was never a chance to find out because the boys decided to use the ice as a target, and it was soon smashed into smithereens.

**Ice tobogganing** If your children have their sled at the ready, waiting eagerly for a snowfall that doesn't come, perhaps they should try the excitement of ice tobogganing. During a bitterly cold family walk, the children wondered why their dad had bothered to bring the sled along when there was not so much as a single flake of snow on the ground. They saw why when they reached the top of a steep slope and, clambering onto the sled as instructed, found themselves sliding at incredible speed across the frozen ground. With

**Ice monsters** Several children might work together to shape an ice monster that creeps across the frozen landscape. Try using ice pieces in different ways to create three-dimensional dinosaurs, dragons, or other monsters, adding pebble eyes or fir-cone ears to bring them more alive.

**Ice pictures** Having smashed all the ice in a frozen puddle, Jake decided to collect the broken pieces and put them to good use. By carefully arranging the differently sized sections he managed to create a collage of an ice man (pictured right). Ice can be used to make all sorts of pictures on the ground or on tree stumps or rocks.

screams of delight and excitement they reached the bottom and immediately climbed back up for another go. This activity is fast and exhilarating, and can only be done when the ground is frozen rock hard. Children should be closely supervised; frozen ground is unforgiving.

## BUILDING WITH ICE

**Ice stacks and monuments** Try building an ice stack by slowly piling slabs of ice on top of each other, using the largest pieces at the bottom. The children may even be able to make an arch by creating two ice stacks side by side, then very slowly and carefully tilting them toward each other. Alternatively, try piling pieces of ice into a heap to make an ice monument.

**Ice castles** Inspired by the discovery of a winter stream in which every twig was coated with a fine layer of crystal-clear ice, some children on a winter holiday decided to build a magical castle fit for an ice queen. Using a pile of rocks on a grassy bank as a starting point, they added pieces of ice and ice-coated twigs to create a glistening fortress.

**Icicle creations** The discovery of icicles is usually accompanied by great delight—they are just asking to be snapped off and played with. An icicle can be stuck in the ground to make a tower for an ice castle or used as a unicorn's horn in an imaginary game. Those wanting a real creative challenge could try stringing several icicles together to make a mobile or attaching icicles onto ice or stone by melting one end slightly with a warm hand and then allowing the icicle to refreeze on the surface.

### SAFETY TIPS
- Always keep away from ice that has formed over deep water.
- Make sure children are wrapped up warm and wearing gloves when they handle ice.
- Be careful with sharp icicles.
- Watch out for very slippery ice.

# ICE MOBILES

During a walk one winter's day an observant child noticed fallen leaves and seeds trapped in the sheets of ice that had formed over puddles in the track. Breaking off a piece frozen around a leaf, she held it up to the light to see a beautiful stained-glass effect.

Inspired by this discovery, the family returned home to have a go at making frozen mobiles to hang outside the kitchen window. They found that encasing natural materials such as berries and seeds in ice revealed them in new and unexpected ways. The family enjoyed watching the mobiles as they slowly melted away over the next few days.

## MAKING THE MOBILES

This winter activity needs a stretch of very cold weather. Make the mobiles on a night when a cold frost is forecast.

• Ask each of the children to choose a few favorite things from their collection of natural materials.

• Put the chosen items inside pastry cutters placed in saucers or plastic bowls, or arrange them in upturned jam-jar lids.

• Carefully place the containers in a row on a tray.

• Lay a piece of string along the row of containers, linking them together. The string must go right into each pastry cutter or jam-jar lid to ensure it will be frozen into the mobile.

• Pour water into each container, making sure all the materials and pieces of string are submerged.

• If the temperature outside is below freezing, place the tray outdoors where it will not be disturbed.

• If the temperature outside is above freezing, remember you can always cheat by placing the mobile in the freezer.

• When the mobiles have frozen, carefully remove the icy discs from their containers. You may need to use a little warm water to loosen the ice and release the pastry-cutter shapes.

• Hang your mobiles just outside a window or on a tree in the garden, and enjoy them for as long as the cold weather lasts.

**WHAT YOU NEED**
- Seasonal materials collected during a winter's walk. They might include evergreen leaves and needles, last autumn's fallen leaves, berries and seeds, or perhaps some of next spring's catkins or snowdrops.
- Several saucers, plastic bowls, or jam-jar lids
- Metal pastry cutters of various shapes
- A tray
- String
- A freezer—in case it's not cold enough outside

# SNOW SCULPTING

Great excitement greets winter's first snowfall—among children if not adults. If snow arrives in school time, the teachers may as well stop talking. The children's eyes will be fixed on the windows, as they try to see if the swirling flakes will settle or just melt away. They will be desperate to get out in the snow, to be the first to leave their tracks in the pristine whiteness, to build snowmen, pelt each other with snowballs, or slide downhill on a sled or a plastic bag. But snow brings other opportunities too, such as a chance to spy on the activities of wild animals and birds that leave telltale tracks or to try one's hand at shaping snow into weird and wonderful sculptures.

Even a walk through snow is an adventure. On one memorable day, several families met up for a long walk through a fresh fall of snow. The children made ice sculptures, jumped into drifts, used their hands and even faces to leave prints, and lay down on their backs and scraped their arms through the snow to create snow angels. Try going out after dark and let the children run through an eerily light, snow-covered landscape.

## SNOW CREATURES

Why is it that everyone always builds snowmen? Why not snow women or snow children or even snow animals? With a little imagination, all sorts of creatures can be shaped out of snow, using natural materials such as twigs, stones, leaves, and icicles to add those defining details.

My son and his friend were hugely disappointed when winter's first, and perhaps only, snowfall was far too fine and powdery for making decent snowballs. Not to be outdone, they soon found another use for it. They had a lot of fun working together to create a snow mouse and hedgehog (pictured right) in a local park. Following their example, two little girls used a pair of antlers they found at the back of a garage to transform a heap of snow in the garden into a reindeer.

An alternative way to make snow creatures and other sculptures is to use packed snow, which provides a firmer material much more suitable for carving. Make packed snow by compressing it into a plastic storage box and then tipping it out to form a square building block ready to sculpt. Encourage the children to use beach spades, garden trowels, or even spoons to carve castles, geometric shapes, or whatever they are inspired to create.

## GIANT SNOWBALLS

There is something immensely satisfying about rolling a little snowball over and over across the snow-covered ground, watching it get bigger and bigger until it is so huge it can barely be pushed along. Giant snowballs can be used in several different ways:

- Try carving and molding with hands or a beach spade and spoon to create a snow person or animal.

- Several giant snowballs rolled together in a circle might be used to make a den.

- The children can decorate snowballs, covering them in materials such as mud, leaves, or twigs to create natural sculptures.

- As a snowball is rolled, it leaves behind a grassy trail through the snow. If the children plan their rolling route they can make a pattern in which exposed grass contrasts with the snow.

## SNOW TUG-OF-WAR

For a tug-of-war with a difference, try building a snow wall in an open space, with a rope running through the middle of the wall. If a team on each side of the wall pulls hard on the rope, one group of children will eventually crash into the soft, snowy barrier.

**SAFETY TIPS**
- Make sure children are wrapped up warm and wearing gloves when they play in the snow.
- Watch out for slippery ice.

## SNOW DENS

Igloos hold a great fascination for children, who want to know how they are made and how on earth anyone inside might keep warm. If there is a reasonably heavy fall of snow, they will enjoy trying to build their own igloo or snow den. Jo's children built a den from snow bricks compressed in a plastic box. They built three walls with the bricks, leaving a couple of gaps for windows, then used a sheet of plywood for the roof. Although the finished den wasn't a particularly inviting place, the planning and building of it had been an enjoyable challenge. Visiting the den after dark, the children found that someone had left a burning candle inside, which made the place seem more welcoming and provided an insight into how cozy an igloo home could be.

Gone home     This way     Not this way

# WILD TRACKING

Many a reluctant walker has been encouraged on his or her way by looking out for signs to follow, whether they are the spots or arrows of a permanent nature trail, deer tracks through the mud, or a succession of twig arrows laid on the ground. Wild tracking is a game of hide-and-seek with a difference, in which excited children seek out a trail left by their friends as they try to discover where they might be hiding.

This activity was very popular at one children's event held in a wooded country park. Groups of up to thirty children were split into two teams (trailblazers and trackers), each accompanied by two adults. The trailblazers would dash off to lay a trail through the woods, choosing a complex route and putting down false trails now and again. Once they had found a good hiding place, they would hide as quietly as they could. The trackers then had to put their observation skills to the test, searching for arrows and any other clues that might lead them to their quarry. Once the trailblazers had been found, the teams would swap roles.

## PLAYING WILD TRACKING

This game can be played with any number of children and is a great way to make family walks more exciting. It should be played in woodland, scrub, or perhaps a park—anywhere with a reasonable amount of cover for hiding in and a good network of paths to follow.

Ask the children to shape natural materials, such as sticks, grass, stones, chalk, or whatever else might be found, into a series of arrows on the ground. You may wish to agree on a trail code so everyone will be able to read it. This code could include the following:

**Arrow** Indicates which direction to go.

**Cross** Indicates the dead end of a false trail.

**Triangle** Indicates that the trail could be along one of two paths.

**Arrow placed over a stick** Indicates that the trackers should go over an obstacle in the path (such as a fallen tree).

**Arrow with two arrowheads** Indicates that the trailblazing party has split.

• Ask the trailblazers to run ahead to lay their trail, continuing until they reach a suitable hiding place where they will lie in wait for the trackers. They must leave a clear trail with plenty of arrows,

**Party split up**

**Turn left or right**

**Water in this direction**

particularly at tricky spots where several paths meet or where the route is overgrown.

- The trackers should wait for ten to fifteen minutes before setting off to follow the trailblazers; this should give the trailblazers plenty of time to get a good head start. The trackers then follow the trail until they track down their quarry.

- Once the trailblazers have been caught, the teams should change roles.

**Flour trail** During one outdoor children's party, one of the adults rushed ahead through the woods, scattering flour on the ground and hurling it at tree trunks to leave a clear, biodegradable trail for everyone else to follow. Chaos reigned as ten excited boys dashed after their prey, following the trail until they discovered him hiding in the bushes. (Don't use non-biodegradable materials to make trails unless you can collect everything afterward.)

**SAFETY TIPS**
- Make sure each group of children is accompanied by at least one adult.
- Only use paths with public access.
- When playing tracking games with many children, encourage the children to get into pairs and stay with their partner at all times.
- Walkie-talkies can be useful, allowing the teams to contact each other if necessary.

**Tracking down treasure** Instead of there being two teams of children, an adult could go ahead and lay a trail, hiding some "treasure" at the end of it. This activity can be organized before an expedition, the route being selected to coincide with a planned walk or to lead the children in a circle so they finish near where they began. This version of wild tracking is better for younger children; older children enjoy the excitement and freedom of laying their own trail.

# WIND FLAGS

The wild winter wind is noisy, cold, and even a little frightening as it rushes past and howls through the trees, ripping off leaves and branches. Yet children also find it thrilling and exhilarating to run along a hilltop as the wind steals away the sounds of their excited screams, to lean into the wind and feel its force support their body, or to walk in the woods listening as the wind whips through the trees. A walk on a wild and windy day can be a great experience for all the family, provided everybody is wrapped up warm.

Although flying a kite is synonymous with windy days, small children can't really feel any degree of control over a distant diamond in the sky. Wind flags are a child-friendly alternative, making the noise and movement of the wind much more immediate. The flags shown on this page were made with great anticipation by children eager to get outside for a windy adventure on the local hillside. They enjoyed the flags for weeks afterward, using them for games of flag raiding and for asserting ownership of their camps. This straightforward activity appeals to a wide age range but is particularly good for very young children, who find the flags easy to control.

## MAKING WIND FLAGS

These flags were made at home from brightly colored cotton. Crêpe paper can also be used, but is less suitable for very windy days.

• Let the children choose their own fabric, then help them to cut it into long triangular shapes. The longer the tail on the flag, the more the children will be able to see and feel the wind.

• Attach the fabric to the sticks using a stapler, a needle and thread, or a hot-glue gun (the latter should only be used by adults).

• Decorate the flag with scraps of fabric or color it with pens or paints.

• Go outside to any large, open space, preferably an exposed hillside so the children can enjoy being up high in the wind. Let them run, march, or dance along with their flags flapping behind them.

• Those who wish to create a more dramatic flag can draw a design on a triangular piece of old cotton sheet and color it brightly with paints. The flag can be mounted on a long stick from which the bark has been removed. Then, armed with their flags, the children can set off on an adventure to discover and claim some unknown territory . . .

### WHAT YOU NEED
• Sturdy sticks about 3½ feet (1 m) long, with blunt ends
• Lengths of fine, brightly colored cotton/crepe paper
• Stapler/needle and thread/hot-glue gun
• Scraps of fabric and pens/paints

## CAPTURE THE FLAG

Older children might use their flags for a game of capture the flag.

• Find a large, open space and split the children into two teams.

• Each team should choose an area as a base camp.

• The teams should each use one large flag to mark their base camp. (If they wish, they could have a few smaller flags too.)

• Team members try to steal the flag from the other team's base, but also need to guard their own camp.

• The winning team is the first to capture the other team's flag. (The game needs some careful refereeing!)

# NATURAL DECORATIONS

It is said that the German reformer Martin Luther created the very first Christmas tree after noticing stars twinkling through the branches of a fir; inspired by the combination of lights and greenery, he took a tree indoors and decorated it with candles. All over the world, coniferous trees are harvested and brought inside for festive dressing at Christmas, and it is also becoming increasingly popular to festoon garden trees with strings of lights.

Christmas is a time of excitement and magic, eagerly anticipated by children, but it is also a time of mass consumption and wastefulness. Each year glossy magazines feature elaborately decorated homes, and the shops are piled high with baubles and fairy lights, encouraging us to rush out and purchase the latest look. Yet despite the pressure to buy manufactured decorations, the use of plants such as holly and ivy has remained popular; when other plants are dead or dormant, evergreens provide a potent symbol of continuity.

Many natural materials can be used to make decorations for a winter festival. Homemade baubles and wreaths, angels and candleholders are just some of the ornaments that children might create. Use them to dress a traditional Christmas tree or a favorite tree or shrub in the garden, or try stringing them up in a window.

## MAKING STARS

**Twig stars** The simple five-pointed stars pictured left are each constructed from one long leafless winter twig:

- Bend a supple twig in four places to create five equal lengths.

- Fold it at each bend to create a five-pointed star.

- Tie the two loose ends together with fine wire.

### WHAT YOU NEED

- Begin collecting natural materials during autumn and store in a cool, dry place until December. Suitable items include: twigs; teasels; poppy seedheads; tree seeds such as acorns, maple seeds, or sycamore seeds; fir and pine cones; crab apples; rose hips; cotoneaster, holly, and hawthorn berries; greenery from ivy, holly, and other evergreen trees; mistletoe; feathers.
- Non-natural materials might include: wire; glass jars and night-lights; raffia or string; ribbons; silver or gold glitter spray.
- Scissors/shears
- Glue

- Decorate the star with silver or gold spray, or twist a ribbon or a length of ivy around it.

- Use the stars individually to decorate a Christmas tree or tie them to twigs to make star mobiles.

**Natural colors** Twigs can vary considerably in color, from the yellow of willow to the grey of ash and the deep red of dogwood. Peeling a twig will reveal bare wood in a contrasting color. You can use these natural variations in color to create a range of different stars, perhaps experimenting with twigs cut from shrubs and trees in the garden.

**Stick stars** If you can't find flexible twigs, or find it a little tricky to make the twig stars, try arranging five sticks of similar length and thickness into a star shape and binding them together at each point with fine wire.

## CHRISTMAS LIGHTS

Glass jars decorated with natural materials make unusual seasonal candle holders, suitable for hanging from a tree or placing on a windowsill.

- Wind some fine wire around the top of a jar, securing it in place just below the rim. Then attach another piece of wire across the top of the jar to make a handle.

- Decorate the jars with seeds, ivy, mistletoe, holly, or other suitable natural materials, glued or tied on with raffia.

- Place a night-light in each jar and carefully hang the Christmas lights from a branch outdoors, or place them on a flat surface indoors.

## HONESTY ANGEL

The purple-flowered money plant grows in many gardens but can also be found flourishing on waste ground and roadsides. Its round, semi-transparent seedpods were used to make the angel pictured opposite.

- Make a triangle by bending a twig in two places and securing the ends with wire.

- Attach a poppy seedhead to the apex of the triangle.

- Glue honesty seeds together to make the dress, and fix this to the twig triangle.

- Arrange more honesty seeds in the shape of wings and glue them to a twig. Then attach the twig to the top of the triangle, just below the poppy seedhead.

- A halo made from a piece of honesty seed can be attached with very fine wire.

## SEED DECORATIONS

Seeds, berries, and cones of different sizes and colors provide the perfect raw materials for a whole range of decorations. You will need wires of different thickness. The decorations photographed for this chapter include the following:

**Seed and berry rings** Collect various seeds and berries from hedges and the garden, and thread or glue them onto fine wire. Then bend the wire carefully into the shape of a ring.

**Berry spiral** Thicker wire can be wound around a broom handle to make a spiral and berries threaded onto the wire.

**Berry baubles** These are made by threading different combinations of berries or seeds onto lengths of wire.

**Mystery animals** See what weird and wonderful creatures children can create from seeds, berries, cones, greenery, and some silver and gold spray.

## DECORATING TREES

Homemade decorations look festive on a Christmas tree indoors, but might also be used in other ways.

**African Christmas tree** On a December holiday with friends in Botswana, my children noticed some unusual Christmas trees. Bare branches and twigs were carefully arranged in pots and dressed with a mixture of traditional decorations and natural materials such as seedpods and dried flowers. If any garden trees or shrubs need pruning in the winter, save a few branches and bring them indoors to create your own version of an African Christmas tree, using as many natural decorations, and materials such as cones and seeds, as possible.

**Tree dressing** There are ancient customs originating all over the world in which people celebrate the environmental and cultural value of trees by adorning them with ribbons, lights, and any other decoration that might draw attention to them. Trees may be dressed at different times of year, during the late autumn for example, to celebrate the gathering of harvest, or at the mid-winter solstice, in anticipation of the rebirth of the coming spring. Perhaps homemade, natural decorations along with a few ribbons could be used to dress up a favorite tree in your garden or on a local walk.

**SAFETY TIP**
- Children should always be well supervised when near candles.
- Keep candles away from foliage.

# ALL YEAR
# ROUND

# FUN AT ANY TIME OF YEAR

This book is all about getting outside to enjoy wild places at any time of year, at any time of day, and in any kind of weather. Although some activities are related to seasonal characteristics—spring's new life, summer's lush growth, autumn's fruitfulness, or winter's dormancy—many others can be enjoyed all year round. Trees can always be climbed, rocks scrambled over, and water paddled in. Natural materials such as mud, stones, sticks, and dead leaves will always be available. It is also well worth trying certain activities, such as going to the beach, during what might at first seem the wrong time of year.

One icy winter weekend when they were very young, my children insisted on going to the beach. Undeterred by the layer of frost coating the sand, they had a brief but exhilarating play. Similarly, a group of twelve-year-old girls set off on a sponsored walk one very wet spring day. We expected them to come home early but instead they did the full walk, returning soaked to the skin but full of fun despite, or perhaps because of, the rain. If children are properly dressed they can appreciate all weathers and enjoy the experience of spinning round in the rain with tongues out to catch the drops or flying kites in a wild wind or running through a blizzard.

Children love to return to a familiar, favorite place, whether it is somewhere they can run about and explore, a climbing tree, or a special hidey-hole. By revisiting places as the year moves round, they will experience at first hand how the area changes from day to day, through the seasons, and over the years. They will notice that some things are permanent but others change according to the seasons or the weather. They might observe subtle differences, such as the thickening of a tree canopy as spring becomes summer, or more dramatic change, such as a dry, empty streambed that becomes a rushing torrent after a heavy rainfall.

This chapter includes a range of games and adventures to try out at almost any time of the year. Like many of the activities in this book, they can be repeated in different seasons and in a variety of locations.

# TREE CLIMBING

If we ask Edward where he'd like to go for a walk, he invariably wants to visit one of his two favorite climbing trees. His favorite tree is an ancient, pollarded beech with smooth, grey bark. Situated at the top of a steep, grassy slope, its twisted, tangled branches offer numerous places for him to perch, completely surrounded, in the middle of summer, by a dense canopy of leaves. His second favorite is a tall, slender, silver birch with a ladder of regularly placed branches all the way up its smooth trunk. He climbs as high as he dares, hugging the white bark as he listens to the rattling of leaves in the wind, feeling exhilaration and perhaps just a little fear as the tree sways from side to side.

## FINDING A SPECIAL TREE

Children have always enjoyed climbing trees. A good climbing tree is a real find. It's a place for all sorts of games and adventures and it's also somewhere to sit quietly and enjoy the sounds, sights, and scents of the natural world. Frequent visits will show how the tree changes through the seasons, from the bare branches and open views of winter to the full green camouflage of summer. Climbing a variety of trees, children might begin to notice how different they are and will perhaps be inspired to find out more.

**Troll Tree** When Jake and Dan were very young, they loved to visit the Troll Tree. They would rush up to the ancient, twisted tree with great excitement and some fear, knocking on the bark to scare away the troll before squirming inside the hollow trunk. In the heart of the old tree, they would imagine the troll watching them through the darkness. Hollow trees always have a particular appeal for children; mine were fascinated, and a little horrified, to discover that an enormous hollow baobab tree they saw in Africa had been used as a prison cell for many years.

**SAFETY TIPS**
- Children should only attempt to climb reasonably mature trees with sturdy branches.
- Do not let children climb along dead branches.
- Limit the number of children climbing any one tree.
- Encourage climbers to stay close to the trunk of a tree.

**The One Tree** A friend told us about The One Tree, which stood midway along one of the family's favorite walks. It provided a focus for their outings, a place where the children could stop and play among the tangled roots or clamber into the branches. For very young children a tree such as this can turn into a real friend, whom they love to return to, and they will become familiar with every nook and cranny.

**Fallen trees** A huge, fallen tree is like an adventure playground, providing places to balance and swing, hide and make dens.

# WILD DENS

Imagine being out in the wilderness, completely on your own, forced to find a way to survive. The children's book *Hatchet*, by Canadian author Gary Paulsen, describes how a twelve-year-old city boy, escaped from a crashed airplane, manages to live in the wild. Left with only the clothes he is wearing and a hatchet, the boy learns how to survive. He builds a shelter to protect himself from the elements and wild animals, he finds out how to make fire, and he constructs a bow and arrow to catch food. Although he longs to be rescued, he also learns to love and respect the environment that sustains him. The book appeals to the adventurous instinct of children, and somehow makes games such as den building seem a little more real.

Children find something thrilling in creating their own special place, somewhere on their scale where the grown-ups can't go. Making dens usually involves taking the sofa apart, or draping old blankets over upturned chairs, but children also love to build outdoor dens. Our children teamed up with their friends next door to make a den in the big evergreen hedge separating our front gardens. They clipped away at the inside of the hedge until they had made a secret hideaway large enough for all four of them. Passersby were surprised to hear children's voices coming from inside what looked like an ordinary hedge!

Intrepid explorers might venture into the forest to create a real shelter, sturdy enough to last for some time and solid enough to protect against the elements, providing somewhere to share rations and to return to again and again. The den pictured here gave hours of entertainment, from the careful planning, to the collection of logs, sticks, and blackberry runners, to the supervised construction. And for weeks afterward it was the focus for numerous expeditions: the children made repairs, had picnics there, and used it in all sorts of imaginary games. This was their space, which they had created deep within the woods, and being in it gave them a great sense of belonging.

There is always eager anticipation involved in building a den—much talk of staying there overnight, coping with the elements, and trying to survive in the wilderness. Children will work together excitedly to find suitable materials and create a hideout, but with adult supervision a much stronger shelter can be created. It may even be good enough for you all to spend a night there together, to share a brief experience of living in the wild, surrounded by the noises of the forest.

## SELECTING A SITE

When choosing the location for a den, consider the following:

- The "forest" might be in the back garden or a local park, but woodland provides much more excitement and a real sense of wildness.

- Try to avoid causing too much disturbance to ground flora or animals by finding a place where the woodland floor is relatively bare of plants.

- Make sure there is plenty of suitable dead wood in the area. The building materials for dens are logs, branches, sticks, and leaf litter collected from the woodland floor.

- Try to find a natural feature that could be used as a starting point for the den, such as a large, dead log or a leaning branch. This is much easier than building something from scratch and produces a sturdier structure.

- Avoid hollows, which may become very wet if it rains.

- Avoid building beneath a dense canopy of leaves as they will continue to drip for a long time after a heavy rainfall.

**WHAT YOU NEED**

This activity is about using what you can find. All you need to take with you is some old gloves and maybe a sharp knife, plus resourcefulness and lots of imagination.

## CONSTRUCTING A DEN

The construction of the basic framework, which may involve moving heavy branches, is best done under close adult supervision; it is important that the structure is very strong and reliable. As with the den illustrated here, you could use a fallen log as the starting point and construct the structure following these basic instructions:

- Collect three long branches from the forest floor to form the basic structure. Bind them together firmly at the apex with string or stems such as blackberry runners, honeysuckle, or wild clematis.

- Secure additional branches along one long side to make a framework, again binding them in place with natural materials found nearby.

- Weave smaller twigs and stems through the framework to create a lattice. This must provide a firm mesh suitable for supporting a thatch of leaf litter and grasses.

- Collect leaves and grasses and lay them over the lattice, starting at ground level and working upward. The thick leaf litter of forest floors provides an ideal thatching material, which will insulate and keep out the worst of the rain.

- The finer details will depend on the children. They may, for example, wish to sweep the floor to clear a smooth place to sit with their friends, or to build up layers of leaf litter to create a soft bed.

- Completion can be marked by a brew-up or a celebratory picnic in the new den.

### SAFETY TIPS

- Children should only use knives under careful adult supervision.
- Watch out for plants with thorns and prickles—gardening gloves are very useful for protecting hands.
- Do not light open fires in the forest (see page 187).

## BREWING UP WITH A KELLY KETTLE

Jo's children always enjoy using a Kelly or volcano kettle to make tea or soup. They collect dry leaves and twigs to make a tiny fire in the small metal container that forms the base of the kettle. As soon as the fire has been lit, a hollow metal jacket is placed over the container, enclosing the fire safely. The water, contained within the hollow metal jacket, is heated rapidly as the fire is drawn up through the chimney. Kelly kettles become hot very quickly and should only be used under strict adult supervision. This is the only safe way of lighting a fire in the woods, however, and the small fire is easily extinguished once the water has boiled.

# WOODY BUG HUNTS

Connie used to love finding woodlice beneath rotting logs and watching their tank-like bodies and twitching antennae as they scuttled about looking for darkness. Her favorites were the aptly named pill woodlice, the black ones that curled up into tight little balls when she poked them with her finger. Woody bug hunts help children to discover more about the multitudes of little creatures living in the nooks and crannies of a forest, park, or garden. This activity can be done at most times of the year, except during the coldest winter months.

A multilayered woodland habitat provides all sorts of places for small creatures to find a home, whether up in the tree branches, among the lower-growing shrubs, in the small plants on the ground, in deep layers of leaf litter, or in rotting wood. Each habitat will contain different invertebrate species adapted to life in those particular surroundings. The most accessible places to search for woodland minibeasts are beneath logs, in leaf litter, and in rotting wood. The creatures living here play a key role in the cycle of life, helping to break down dead plant material and releasing trapped nutrients back to the soil, where they will help the next generation of plants to grow strong. Look out for scuttling black ground beetles, woodlice resembling little armored tanks, the many-legged centipedes and millipedes, and the fierce-looking, but harmless, earwigs with their pincerlike tails.

## MINIBEASTS IN LEAF LITTER

- Collect a heap of rotting leaves from the woodland floor and place them on the plastic sheet.

- Carefully sift through the leaves. Children may prefer to wear gloves or use a stick to do this.

- Look very carefully for little creatures, placing them carefully in a bug box or plastic container for further investigation. Use the paintbrush to pick up the smallest.

- When you have completed your investigation, using a magnifying glass and perhaps a field guide, replace all the leaf litter and woodland creatures where you found them.

**WHAT YOU NEED**
- Large plastic sheet
- Gloves (gardening gloves are best)
- Bug boxes/white plastic containers
- Paintbrush
- Magnifying glasses
- Field guide (if required)

**SAFETY TIP**
Make sure the children wash their hands thoroughly with soap after handling woodland debris.

## UNDER LOGS AND BRANCHES

Look for slugs and snails, centipedes and millipedes, woodlice and ground beetles in the dark dampness beneath fallen logs and branches.

- Lift logs gently to investigate underneath, and always return them to their original position.

- Encourage children to leave habitats exactly as they were found.

## IN ROTTEN WOOD

During a camouflage game, these children were distracted by a large log. They poked at the decomposing wood and were surprised to discover that it was as soft as a sponge, more like soil than the hard texture they had been expecting.

- Find a rotting log and see how many different types of creature are living under, on, or inside it.

- Discuss with the children how the rotting wood will eventually be returned to the soil, the nutrients becoming available to the roots of living trees.

# BLINDFOLD ADVENTURES

We observe the natural world predominantly with our eyes, noticing shapes, textures, colors, and contrasts; our other senses usually refuse to play their full part unless forced to do so. Without sight, however, our perception of sounds and smells and our sense of touch are greatly intensified, as if the lack of one sense enhances the others. Blindfolded, we might feel the difference in temperature as we walk from open sunlight into the shade, or hear more clearly the sounds of leaves crackling underfoot, or notice the sweet musty smell of wet leaves.

Traditional blindfold games, such as pin-the-tail-on-the-donkey, remain popular with young children. Unlike adults, who are often slightly anxious when blindfolded, children seem to find the experience fun and exciting. Try taking blindfold games out into the countryside, park, or garden, helping children to enjoy the natural world in new and unexpected ways.

## TREE HUGGING

We may appreciate the shade that trees provide, enjoy their autumn colors, and take pleasure in climbing up into their branches, but it is still easy to take these woodland giants for granted. Tree hugging is a symbol of respect and veneration, often associated with the attempts of environmental activists to protect threatened trees. When children come across trees like the Californian redwood, they need very little encouragement to hug them and find out how many people with outstretched arms it takes to reach all the way around the trunk.

Tree hugging is one way to encourage children to explore the characteristics of different trees, letting their fingertips discover how each tree has its very own texture, shape, size, and personality. This game is suitable for playing in any forest or urban

**WHAT YOU NEED**
- Blindfolds, such as scarves or the eye-shades provided on long-haul flights. Always keep a few blindfolds in your adventure bag—these games are easy to set up and can be enjoyed over and over again in many different places.
- A long, strong rope (if playing rope trails)

park where a variety of trees of different shapes and sizes can be found growing in an area with little or no undergrowth.

- Organize the children into pairs; each child will get a chance to act as guide and to be blindfolded.

- An adult should demonstrate the activity by leading a blindfolded child to a tree and talking him or her through the experience.

- Children acting as guides should hold their partner's forearm firmly and lead him or her carefully to a tree, avoiding any obstacles en route. It is important that the blindfolded children relax into the walk, have trust in their guides, and feel confidence in what their other senses will allow them to perceive.

- The guides should help the blindfolded children explore their trees, guiding their hands to feel if the bark is smooth or fissured, to explore little nooks and crannies, and to touch a bud, an unfurling leaf, a catkin, or a seed.

- The children could also wrap their arms all the way around the trunk, measuring its girth and reaching for limbs branching off the main trunk.

- Ask the children to feel the ground around the tree, searching for fallen leaves and seeds, as well as roots or a cushion of velvety moss.

- The blindfolded children could also use their noses and smell different parts of the tree.

- Once the blindfolded children know their trees, they should be led away by a roundabout route and then spun around a couple of times until they have lost their sense of direction.

- Ask the children to remove their blindfolds and find their trees—they will be thrilled to recognize the right one.

- The children must swap roles so that they all get at least one turn at leading and one at being led.

## GUIDED WALK

In this activity, a blindfolded child is led on a short walk.

- The guide should try to choose an interesting and varied route, along which he or she can direct the blindfolded partner's hands to feel natural objects, such as a smooth cushion of moss, threads of lichen on a branch, some spongy decomposing wood, or the cold face of a rock.

- Add to the experience by providing other natural objects to feel. Can the children identify the shape and texture of a feather, an acorn, a fir cone, or wet mud?

- Crush wild herbs, such as marjoram, thyme, or mint, or other scented plants like hedge garlic or pine needles, and allow the children to smell them and guess what they might be.

- Take the children across different surfaces, such as grass, leaves, a gravel path, or a muddy puddle.

- Try a barefoot trail across dew-laden grass, a mossy bog, or a bed of leaves; this can be an exciting and fun experience but watch out for sharp stones, sticks, and thorns.

## ROPE TRAILS

During a spring expedition to a favorite wild place, a family friend laid a long rope down a steep, grassy hillside, stationing himself at the top to anchor the rope. The children ran down to the bottom, donned blindfolds, and, grabbing onto the rope, hauled themselves up the hill. There were squeals of delight as they negotiated anthills, rabbit holes, and tangled shrubs.

• Successful rope trails require a little planning. The blindfolded children then take turns following the trail, holding onto the rope, which can be secured at various points along the chosen route.

• Make a trail in an area where there is a variety of obstacles to overcome and different terrain to experience. Perhaps the route could go both up- and downhill, follow a shaded woodland path, and cross a sunny clearing, require the children to crawl under low-growing branches and climb over a mossy tree stump, and finally finish up in a deep mound of leaves or even a muddy puddle.

• Add interest by fixing the rope at different levels along the route, sometimes high up and sometimes near the ground.

• An alternative to the fixed rope trail is the moving trail, in which an adult holds one end of the rope and blindfolded children are placed at regular intervals along its length, holding on firmly with one hand. The adult then walks along, pulling the children and warning them about obstacles. The rope should be kept taut and no one should pull on it suddenly. Try leading the children to a secret destination, then removing the blindfolds to see if they can find their way back to the starting point.

# SCAVENGER HUNTS

"Who can find the most unusual thing in these woods today?" Thus began a lively hunt as the children sought high and low for the most weird and wonderful natural objects they could possibly find. After about twenty minutes, their collected treasures included a red kite's feather, snail shells, acorns and pinecones, and, most exciting of all, the rather disgusting remains of a fox's foot. There was much discussion about what the children thought unusual and why, leading to further hunts for yet more unusual treasures.

## ORGANIZING A SCAVENGER HUNT

Looking for items on a scavenger list should encourage children to be observant and think creatively. Young children might be asked to look for five different leaves, a feather, and a fir cone, something white, and something fluffy. Older children might be given a more challenging list, perhaps being asked to search for a sun-trap, a seed that catches a lift, the remains of an animal's meal, something that protects a plant, and an animal's hair.

• Discourage the collection of wildflowers.

• Once everyone has made their collection, gather together to share discoveries and discuss why certain items were chosen.

• Encourage older children to think about the role their finds may play in nature's processes (nuts, for example, can provide food, while dead leaves enrich the soil).

• Most of the scavenged items will be objects and materials that are found lying around, such as seeds, leaves, feathers, shells, and pebbles. Some of these items are suitable for taking home, perhaps to form the start of a natural history collection or to be used to create a collage or a sculpture of an imaginary creature.

• Ensure that the majority of the scavenged items are left in the environment where they were found.

## DIFFERENT SCAVENGING GAMES

**Instant scavenging** Keep a few ideas up your sleeve for a spontaneous activity to produce if children are flagging or need something new as a focus. They might look for signs of spring, for things they think are useful to humans, for signs of animal activity, for some treasure, or even for something they think is disgusting . . .

**Competitions** Who can be the first to bring back a feather, a shell, or a chewed nut? Who can find the biggest leaf or the snail shell with the most stripes?

**Virtual scavenging** Provide the children with a pencil and a scavenging list that includes things that are impossible to collect physically, such as an oak tree, a rabbit hole, a bird's nest, or an anthill. Ask them to show you each item as they find it.

**Scavenging imaginings** Can they find a fairy's cloak or an elf's table, a hobbit's hole or a dragon's lair? Using ideas from a favorite storybook or film, make up a scavenger hunt that leads their imaginations in search of all sorts of unlikely treasures.

**Miniature scavenging** Provide the children each with a very small container, such as a matchbox or a film container, and ask them to see how many natural things they can fit inside. Send them off to search for tiny items, such as a blade of grass, a pine needle, a small stone, a thorn, or a seed. After about twenty minutes, gather the children together and ask them to tip out their finds onto a piece of paper or card for counting. Perhaps they could try sorting their finds into categories.

**Beach scavenging** Who can find the smallest shell, a mermaid's purse, a pebble with a hole in it, three different types of seaweed, or the most interesting piece of driftwood?

**Odd one out** Provide the children with egg boxes and ask them to collect five similar things and a sixth that is different. It is up to each child to decide what the similarities and differences should be, and up to you and the other children to guess which item is the odd one out.

**Kim's game** This traditional party game can be adapted as a scavenger hunt. Hide a collection of about ten different natural materials beneath a cloth and then show them to the children for a maximum of thirty seconds. Can they remember what they saw? Can they go off and collect the same things?

### WHAT YOU NEED

- Prepared scavenger lists
- Collecting bags/containers, such as yogurt pots or egg boxes. The type of container doesn't really matter, but for the sake of fairness give each child the same sort.

### SAFETY TIPS

- Discourage the collection of berries or toadstools, some of which are poisonous.
- Ensure the children wash their hands thoroughly afterward.

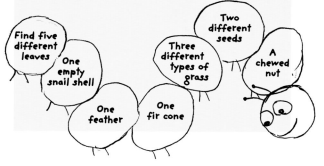

# NATURE DETECTIVES

During a walk in the heart of the African bush, my children were amazed to see how our two local guides solved the clues left behind by the animals. The guides could identify each footprint and every hole in the ground, the remains of plant or animal material told them who had been eating what, and they even knew which animals had left each pile of dung. They could understand signs too subtle for us even to notice: an overturned leaf, a slight compression in the soil, a hair caught on a thorn. They read it all like a newspaper, finding out exactly who was doing what and where, and then took us to the best places to see more wild animals than we'd ever thought possible.

## WHAT YOU NEED

- Magnifying glasses
- Equipment for making plaster casts of animal tracks (see the instructions for making mud casts on page 55)
- Collecting bags/containers
- A field guide to animal tracks and signs

## SAFETY TIP

Do not let children touch droppings with their hands. They can use a stick if they want to try to find out what an animal has been eating.

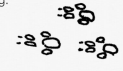

To the uninitiated such clues are an unsolvable puzzle, but an experienced tracker can read them by using all his senses, becoming completely tuned in to the animal he is following. Although it takes years to build up such knowledge and skill, children can be encouraged to be more aware of tracks and signs, so that they too might become nature detectives and spy on the activities of wildlife.

## FINDING AND INTERPRETING TRACKS

On a winter walk, my son's friend wondered who had left all the small, oval tracks crisscrossing the snow. Each set was composed of four footprints repeated in the characteristic pattern made by a rabbit hopping along. The child was intrigued by the sheer number of tracks, indicating just how busy the natural world is when we aren't around. By finding and following tracks, children can get an insight into the lives of birds and animals.

- Tracks are most easily spotted during winter and early spring, when the ground is muddy and there is less vegetation. Look for them on bare, muddy earth, on damp sand and mud near streams or ponds, or in snow.

- The fresher the tracks, the clearer and easier to spot they are; an early-morning tracker will get the best rewards, especially after a fresh snowfall.

- The best light for spotting tracks is in early morning or late evening, when the sun is at a slant and casts deeper shadows.

- Try scattering some sand outside an animal's hole. Return the next day to see if any telltale tracks have been left for you.

Duck      Fox      Dog      Heron      Mouse

- You can get an idea of how quickly an animal was moving when it left tracks: the further apart the prints are, the faster the animal was running.

- Children might try to follow sets of tracks, to see where they go, or they could make plaster casts of them to take home (as described on page 55). By recording tracks in plaster and noting the pattern of the footfalls, it should be possible to discover what type of animal left them.

### ANIMAL PATHWAYS

Many animals are creatures of habit, regularly using the same paths between den and feeding ground. My children found some animal paths in a wood and followed them down a hill and out into a field. We could see what looked like a badger's sett further up the hill, and, although we found no sign of any tracks on the path, we thought it was probably used by badgers going to the field to dig up juicy earthworms.

Children are much better at spotting animal pathways than adults are and they enjoy trying to follow them. Encourage the children to spot the telltale tracks left by animal activities as well as other clues, such as animal hairs caught on a wire fence.

### OTHER CLUES

Some items, such as feathers, food remnants, or droppings, provide hints about the identity of the creature that left them behind.

**Single feathers** Birds molt gradually, losing feathers one at a time as replacements grow. Encourage children to look at the patterns and colors of single feathers and to notice the differences between the soft, downy feathers from a bird's body and the strong flight feathers from a wing. Make a collection of feathers—they can be used for all sorts of creative activities or for making the flights on an arrow.

**Clumps of feathers** Several feathers found in one place may be a sign of predatory behavior. If so, you are likely to find small and large feathers together, along with other more gory remains.

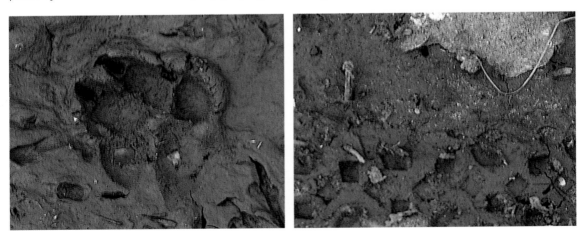

Deer          Horse          Cat          Crow          Rat

**Nuts and seeds** Look under trees for chewed shells of nuts or seeds. Each animal eats them in a slightly different way. Squirrels, for example, break nuts neatly in half but mice or voles gnaw a hole in them.

**Chewed leaves** These might be a sign of a hungry caterpillar or some other insect.

**Chewed cones** Squirrels completely strip all the scales from a cone.

**Bones** Remains of bones may provide evidence of predatory behavior. If bones have been picked clean and bleached in the sun, they can be collected and taken home for identification.

**Eggshells** Birds' eggs are very vulnerable to predators. Children can try making a collection of broken shells of different colors.

**Pellets** Having no teeth, birds must either tear their prey apart or eat it whole, swallowing large quantities of indigestible material such as bones, fur, and feathers. This material is compacted into pellets and coughed up about twice a day. Pellets are produced by gulls, crows, owls, and other birds of prey, and are usually found near nests or below perching or roosting sites. Dry pellets can be pulled apart with tweezers to reveal fur, feathers, bones, pieces of snail shell, and plant fragments.

**Droppings** Given that toilet training figures so large in a two-year-old's life, we shouldn't be surprised that little children are fascinated by "poo." While out on a walk they will spot all sorts of animal "poo," so perhaps their fascination could be put to good use. Many animals and birds produce very distinctive droppings, which trackers and

ecologists use to tell them where a species might be going or what it has been eating. Encourage children to look out for droppings and use a field guide with the older ones to try to identify which animals have been to call.

## ANIMAL HOMES
Youngsters love to spot little holes or nests and speculate about who might live there. Encourage them to look not just at a hole in the ground but also at the area around it to see if there are any other clues, such as prints or the remains of food. Finding answers to the clues left by animals and birds is not easy, but this shouldn't stop children from looking around them and asking questions about who lives where and how they survive.

# PLAYING AROUND WITH BOATS

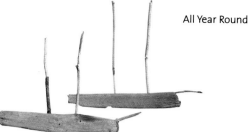

Winnie-the-Pooh invented the game of Pooh-sticks after accidentally dropping a fir cone from the upstream side of a bridge and discovering that it appeared shortly afterward on the downstream side. Using marked sticks instead of fir cones, Winnie-the-Pooh and his friends spent many happy hours playing Pooh-sticks, watching anxiously to see whose stick would emerge first from under the bridge. Even children unfamiliar with A.A. Milne's stories of Winnie-the-Pooh will love to play Pooh-sticks at every bridge they find, and for serious players there is an international Pooh-sticks championship held each spring in England on the River Thames in Oxfordshire, raising funds for the Royal National Lifeboat Institute (RNLI).

Try taking Pooh-sticks a little bit further by encouraging children to make their very own tiny boats out of all sorts of natural materials. The boats can be taken out for adventures at sea, for races down a rocky stream, or for cruises across the paddling pool in the garden.

## RUSH BOATS

Hiking in the mountains, Jo and her family stopped for a rest beside a small stream. The children soon discovered that the rushes growing nearby could float, and they decided to make miniature boats. Rushes grow commonly in damp grassland and moorland, as well as near streams and ponds; a very absorbent lightweight pith inside a tough outer layer makes them both buoyant and strong. The children bound and wove rushes together to make little raftlike boats, which were launched on an adventure down the fast-flowing stream. Running along the bank the children followed the boats on their dangerous journey, egging them on through the obstacles. Try making several little boats to race down a stream. How far will they go? Can they survive the waterfalls? Can they find a way between the rocks?

## BEACH-LITTER BOATS

Boatbuilding is a great project for a family holiday; different age groups will enjoy trying to construct some sort of floating vessel using whatever materials are to hand. Try searching among flotsam and jetsam on a beach for boatbuilding materials such as plastic and driftwood.

This might be a project to work on together, with the challenge of making a boat followed by a sailing expedition through a network of rockpools. Alternatively, perhaps everybody would like to build their own boat in secret. At the end of the holiday, you could hold a launching party to find out whose boat will stay afloat for the longest time or travel the furthest.

Beach-litter boats can also be made at home. Among the various beach treasures scattered in our sand pit, the children came across a pile of cockleshells. These became boats that set sail on a risky journey across the garden pond. After the children had discovered which cockleshells floated best, they loaded smaller shells into the better boats to see how much cargo each could carry before they sank.

## BUILDING BOATS AT HOME

A group of children decided to try making boats from a variety of materials. They checked the seaworthiness of the boats in the paddling pool before taking them out on a serious expedition to a nearby stream—there was fierce debate about the buoyancy of each boat.

- Exactly how the boats are constructed is up to each child, but corks are buoyant and a good starting point if you want to guarantee that every boat will float.

- The basic structure can be decorated and perhaps provided with a sail, which could be a feather or leaf attached using a cocktail stick.

- Try experimenting with a range of natural materials to find out which ones float. Jo's children discovered that hollow stems of reeds float very well, and they lashed them together with grass to make great little rafts.

- Taking the boats to a stream provides a more challenging test: will they be able to withstand a current? Most of the boats pictured opposite proved to be very streamworthy, going on to take part in a fierce battle between two navies.

## FLOATING LEAVES

Children playing in a local stream collected different leaves and put them in the water to see which floated best. There were races and challenges set for each leaf, and comparisons made between those leaves that were tough and waxy and those that were soft. With a little adult help, a water snake (pictured above right) was made by linking leaves together with thread. Grass or thorns could also be used for joining leaves. Try making a very long snake and watching how it moves as it floats downstream.

### WHAT YOU NEED
- Lots of corks
- Feathers and leaves for sails
- The hollow stems of reeds
- Other natural materials, such as twigs, pieces of bark, poppy seedheads, and a few flowers
- Cocktail sticks, glue and modelling clay for joining and sticking materials together

### SAFETY TIPS
- Children should always be well supervised near water.
- It is advisable to sail these boats only on very shallow pools or streams.

# BEACHES THROUGH THE YEAR

The word "beach" is usually associated with hot, lazy days spent basking in the sun and swimming in the sea. Yet children love the seaside at any time of year; they will happily build sandcastles in the rain, run on the sand through the snow, or play in the mud of an estuary. Provided they are wrapped up warm, children enjoy being near the sea in all weathers.

A winter walk along a beach might involve gathering driftwood and finding a sheltered spot to build a fire to make sweet tea or hot chocolate. The making of fires in the countryside is generally to be discouraged, particularly during dry weather, but small fires can be built quite safely on pebbly or sandy beaches using driftwood washed up by the waves. The fire should be built on a rock or among a ring of stones so that there will be no danger of it spreading. (See page 187.)

## MAKING CHARCOAL PENCILS

During one expedition to a stony beach, a fire was built to heat water for a much-needed warm drink. After the children had spent awhile poking long, thin sticks into the embers at the edge of the fire, someone realized they could use the resulting charcoal like a pencil. This was the start of a happy game involving the manufacture of charcoal pencils for drawing pictures and patterns on the rocks.

### SAFETY TIPS
- Wait until the fire has formed a bed of hot embers before allowing children to make charcoal pencils.
- Stay beside the children while they are playing with sticks and fire.
- Afterward, make sure the embers are cold, and leave the site as you found it.

## SEASIDE MOBILES

During an outing to a wild and windswept beach the children collected sea-smoothed driftwood and an assortment of shells, mermaids' purses, and feathers. They insisted on taking these mementos home with them, suspending their favorites from the driftwood to make a seaside mobile. Natural treasures can be collected from the beach at any time of year and used in many creative activities.

# OUTDOOR PARTIES

The long evenings and warm weather of summer make it an easy season to be outside, yet any time can be outdoor party time—provided everyone is prepared for the weather and willing to give it a go. During one of Jake's outdoor parties it began to pour with rain, but the boys were undaunted by the weather. They carried on with their games and later enjoyed storytelling under an improvised shelter. A good time was had by all, in spite of the weather.

crowd of friends, and many of the activities described in this book lend themselves very well to children's parties.

A friend chose to celebrate her fortieth birthday with a large outdoor party at a picnic site in some nearby woods. Lots of families turned up with their picnic rugs, food and wine, baseball bats and Frisbees. The children played happily in the surrounding trees: some built a den and others climbed trees, played hide-and-seek, blew bubbles, or had their faces painted.

Family parties and children's parties can both work well outdoors, but it is important to choose a location where wildlife and other people will not be unduly disturbed by a crowd of chattering adults and excitable children.

One boy with a winter birthday was offered an expensive packaged party by his parents, but what he really wanted was a wild party out in the woods. So that was what they gave him: an afternoon of wild tracking, swinging on a rope strung between two trees, and toasting marshmallows round a fire. The boys all had a great time running around and letting off steam, and the birthday boy saved his parents a small fortune. Children love the opportunity to run free in wild places with a big

## PARTY IDEAS

Here are some suggestions for other types of parties. Night parties are described in the next chapter (see page 168).

**Family walks** Meeting up with a crowd of friends or relatives for a walk can make a great party. Children enjoy walking and running with their friends, especially if there are activities to do on the way. Summer walks could include a picnic or barbecue, and crisp winter walks might be followed by tea and cakes back home.

**Parties at a nature reserve** A friend's daughter celebrated several birthdays at a nature reserve on the edge of the small town where the family live. The girls had a go at pond dipping (see page 42), collected colors (page 74), played blindfold games (page 147), and went on scavenger hunts (page 150).

**Wild tracking parties** These are always very popular but need careful organization and supervision. Children must stay in pairs and not wander away from the trail. (See page 126.)

**Expedition parties** Pack up some ration boxes and send the children off on an expedition to discover something in the woods. Keep an eye on them—perhaps you could ambush them when they least expect it!

**Fairy parties** A group of girls may enjoy a fairy party. Try covering some pebbles in glitter and leaving them in a trail through the woods for the children to follow. Perhaps the trail could end in a clearing where a miniature tea set has been laid out for a fairies' tea party. Some of the games and activities described in this book could be adapted to the fairy

**SAFETY TIPS**

- When taking large groups of children to the countryside or a park, make sure they know who is responsible for them and how they should behave.
- Agree on a meeting point.
- Ask the children to stay in pairs for games where the group may become dispersed.
- As a general rule, don't make fires in wild places (the fire referred to in this chapter was made at a friend's farm). For some tips for the very few occasions when it may be appropriate to have a campfire, see the fire safety rules on page 187.

theme. The children might want to go on a scavenger hunt to find fairy cups, food, and clothes, for example, or create a miniature fairy garden (see page 71).

# AFTER DARK

# FUN AFTER DARK

When Edward and Jake were planning how to celebrate their tenth birthdays, they set their hearts on a nighttime expedition and camping trip. This might not sound like most people's idea of a children's party—particularly as both birthdays are in December. But the discovery of a barn offering dry accommodation on a nearby nature reserve made it all seem possible, and plans were set in motion for what turned out to be one of the most successful and memorable parties our sons have ever had.

Twelve excited boys and several adults gathered about two miles from the barn just as darkness was falling. The children rushed about flashing their torches and calling out to each other; for many of them this was a completely new experience. Once we were deep in the woods, the chattering boys were told to be quiet and to switch off their torches. They soon began to hear owls hooting and mysterious rustlings in the undergrowth, and as their night sight developed they realized they could see pale tree trunks and the chalky track winding ahead.

When we emerged from the woods into open scrub and grassland, the children were encouraged to continue to take their time and to look and listen. One sharp-eyed boy noticed something glowing faintly in the grass, then everyone began to spot the little, luminous lines. We managed to collect one of the glowing objects and under torchlight identified it as a centipede. On closer observation we realized that it wasn't the centipede itself that was luminous, but its secreted slimy trail. When we arrived at the barn, the boys rushed to tell the reserve warden of our find. They were intrigued to discover that although he knew about the centipedes and their strange, luminous secretions, he had not yet identified the name of the species.

All the boys remember the exciting activities of that unusual party—the walk through the dark forest, toasting marshmallows over a fire, the silly party games, and the discovery of those centipedes and their mysterious, luminous trails. Such over-night expeditions are quite an undertaking, but a simple night walk without torches can also be a real adventure. Night transforms the natural world into a very different place; for some children it is a time of excitement and discovery, but for others it is sinister and frightening. Yet darkness itself is not something to be fearful of, and the more children find out about the mysteries of the night, the less scary they will seem.

On a warm summer night moths may be seen darting through the air, and the sea may glow eerily with phosphorescence. The children may notice that the loss of vision seems to magnify the sounds of the night—the croaking of frogs, chirping of crickets, hooting of owls, barking of foxes, or melodic singing of a nightingale. They may also discover that as the quality of light varies, so does the quality of darkness: there is darkness in which the startling brightness of the moon casts shadows, moonless darkness in which the stars shine more brightly, and the enclosing darkness of a damp, foggy night that muffles sounds and shrinks the world.

Most children have few opportunities to experience real darkness because in towns and cities there is no escape from the pervading glare of streetlights. Darkness is generally seen as something that harbors unknown dangers, something to be avoided. Yet a well-supervised nighttime trip to the countryside can be a

captivating experience, and once the children's eyes have adapted to the dark, excitement will begin to replace their fear. It is rewarding to explore the natural world in the dark, even if you are simply finding out which creatures come into the garden at night. Stay close together and be aware that some children might be scared. (You may find that fear of the dark makes unruly children a little easier to contain!) The activities in this section should help children to be less frightened after dark, increase their enjoyment of night's mysteries, and help them to understand the different ways in which nocturnal animals are adapted to cope with darkness.

# NIGHT WALKS

Night walks can be fun at any time of year, but are perhaps most exciting during the spring and summer months. In spring, when the vegetation is not yet very dense, there is more chance of seeing mammals; this is the time to find a hiding place in the woods and look out for families of foxes and badgers. A walk on a still summer's night, on the other hand, is more likely to reveal those mysterious and fascinating flying mammals—bats.

There are other creatures that may also be spotted in the summertime. Driving home after a spectacular fireworks display one warm, still July night, we decided to stop off at a favorite nature reserve for a late-evening walk. As we strolled across the dark hillside, we noticed a pinpoint of green light glowing in the grass. Then we began to see more and more of them, until we were surrounded by an entirely natural display of hundreds of tiny lights. I picked one of them up, showing the children the glowworm's caterpillarlike body. The hind end of its abdomen lit the palm of my hand with an eerie green light; curious faces crowded round, eyes staring in wonder at the little creature. I explained that this was a flightless female using her light to attract a winged male. Glowworms are found in areas of rough and unimproved grassland, and emit light from about two hours after sunset on warm, dry summer nights.

## PREPARING FOR A NIGHT WALK

Although country walks will be darker and wilder, an urban night walk can also be rewarding. Many mammals live in the parks and gardens of towns.

**Planning the route** It is easy to get lost in the dark, so only take children out for night walks along routes you are familiar with. The route does not need to be long, but should allow the children to feel that they really are out in the wilds, or at least away from streetlights. Even a well-known path will seem exciting and new at night, and familiar views look different after dark, with the lights of towns and villages shining all around and the moon rising high in a darkening sky.

**Making a trail** If there is time for someone to walk the route just beforehand, you could mark it with chalked arrows—the children will enjoy searching for these with their torches. Alternatively, try making a trail with glowsticks (these can be purchased from good toyshops).

**Good timing** If you set off at dusk, you will hear and see the arrival of the animal night shift as they emerge from their daytime hiding places.

**Suitable clothing** Wear non-rustling clothes in dark colors. You could add to the excitement of the

### WHAT YOU NEED

- Dark, non-rustling clothes and sensible, soft-soled footwear
- Face paints
- Several torches and spare batteries. Votives placed in jam jars make simple homemade lanterns; to create a handle, attach a length of string to the top of the jar, securing it by winding tightly just below the rim.
- Binoculars for stargazing or looking at the moon
- A picnic and a thermos flask of a warm drink

### SAFETY TIPS

- Make sure everyone stays close together.
- Children should walk slowly and carefully to avoid tripping over hidden obstacles.
- There should always be an adult at the front and at the rear of the group.
- Provide each child with a fluorescent armband or perhaps attach glowsticks to clothing.
- Encourage the children to stay in pairs.
- Children holding candle lanterns must be very carefully supervised.

occasion by suggesting the children camouflage their faces with streaks of charcoal or mud. Wear sensible footwear, with soft soles that will allow you to walk quietly; better still, let the children go barefoot for a while if you feel it is safe for them to do so.

**Night lighting** Red cellophane placed over a torch lens will prevent wild animals from seeing the light.

## DURING THE WALK

**Using night sight** Encourage the children to avoid using their torches as they walk along. Once their eyes have become accustomed to the darkness, they will be amazed by how much they can see.

**Nighttime bugs and beetles** Which little creatures are out and about at night? Small torches can come in very handy for exploring restricted areas—try investigating an old tree stump or an anthill, or searching under a log or stone. Remember to leave all logs and stones as you found them.

**Listening game** Place a lantern on the ground, in the middle of a woodland clearing or other open space, and encourage each child to find his or her own place to sit. They should be able to see the lantern from their chosen spot. Allow them at least five minutes to sit quietly, listening to the noises of the night, then call everyone back to the lantern and sit around it to discuss what you all heard.

**Star and moon gazing** Take some time out to look at the night sky, preferably far away from polluting lights. On holiday in the remote countryside, a night walk revealed more stars than Hannah and Edward had ever imagined—stars beyond stars beyond stars in a vast sky that seemed to go on forever. To really enjoy the sky on a clear night, find an open space where the ground is dry and encourage everyone to lie down like the spokes of a wheel, with heads together in the middle. Lie quietly, looking up at the stars and listening to the night sounds. Pass around a pair of binoculars to get an even better view of some of the constellations or to look at the surface of the moon.

# THE BEACH AT NIGHT

Most families go on a beach holiday at some point in their lives, but how many of them take the opportunity of visiting the beach after dark? A nighttime expedition to a quiet beach will be a real adventure. The sound of the waves will seem louder and more insistent, and perhaps the inky blackness of the sea will be flecked with phosphorescence. Some family friends venturing to their favorite beach one night were amazed to see a string of flickering lights glowing in the sand, a row of little beacons leading them toward the water's edge. Rushing up to one of the lights, they found a candle in a steep-sided hole in the sand. Somebody had obviously spent a long time carving out each hole to create a magical pathway of lights.

### WHAT YOU NEED
- Votives/floating candles and matches
- Spades and trowels
- Jam jars

### SAFETY TIPS
- Children playing on a beach at night need to be kept in a group under close adult supervision at all times.
- Watch out for the tide; children will be less aware of the sea's movements at night. Check the tide timetable before going to the beach and try to choose a night when the tide is going out.
- Carefully supervise children playing near votives or floating candles.

For the rest of the holiday the children demanded to go to the beach every evening. And they always took along a bag of votives or floating candles. The creation of sandcastles, pebble houses, and pools took on a new dimension. All the activities described on the following pages work best in very still conditions. The children will quickly become frustrated if the candles are constantly blown out by the wind.

## GLOWING SAND HOLES
- Make the sand holes below the high-tide line, because damp sand holds its shape.

- Make the holes as deep as you can (but not so deep that they collapse or fill with water). Smooth out the sides with a small spade or a trowel.

- Scatter the holes in a trail leading across the beach, to the water's edge or to your picnic spot. Alternatively, try to make a pattern of holes, maybe a circle or even a word.

- Place a single votive in each hole; small glass jars will keep them sheltered and dry.

- Invite some friends to meet you at the beach and watch their surprise and joy as they are welcomed by a trail of glowing sand holes.

## MORE CANDLE CREATIONS
Alternative uses for candles on a beach include:

**Floating candles** On a very still evening, floating candles placed in natural rockpools will create beautiful reflections. Or perhaps the children could dig a series of little pools in very wet sand, then place a floating candle in each pool.

**Illuminated sandcastles** Imagine a sandcastle glowing with light, fit for a fairy ball. By building a castle out of the damp, firm sand left as the tide goes out, it is possible to create nooks and crannies, tunnels and hollows ready to house night-lights. Perhaps the children could set themselves the challenge of constructing the biggest chamber they possibly can inside a sandcastle, and as darkness falls use night-lights to illuminate the whole chamber with a dazzling brightness. Building such a structure requires time and a great deal of patience; it is a project worthy of a whole afternoon followed by an evening beach party complete with a ceremonial lighting of candles and a picnic.

**Candle-lit cairns** On the expedition photographed here, the children built a series of hollow cairns close to each other in a favorite spot on the beach. Placing night-lights in small glass jars inside each cairn created a stunning effect. Try making a variety of hollow structures.

## CANDLELIT BOATS

It has become a tradition for some family friends, no matter where they go on holiday, to build candlelit boats. The challenge for each family member is to collect materials over the holiday and construct his or her own boat. There is much planning and scheming as bits and pieces are gathered together and boats of all kinds assembled in secret. On the last evening of the holiday there is a ceremonial launching party at the nearest suitable expanse of water, whether it is a rockpool, a pond, a stream, or a swimming pool. The boats are lined up on the shore and a lit votive is placed carefully in each one before it is gently pushed out into the water.

### WHAT YOU NEED
You don't need to take any special materials with you. If this activity is done on holiday there will be limited tools and adhesives available, which means that everyone will just have to use their initiative.

### SAFETY TIP
Children must be well supervised when using votive candles and playing near water.

Everyone then eagerly waits to see whose boat will stay afloat the longest or travel the furthest, or burst into flames.

- You can make the boats from natural and found materials. Try using driftwood and plastic washed up on the beach, twigs and bark from woodland, or orange-juice cartons and corks left over from a picnic (see "Playing around with boats," page 159, for more ideas).

- Any design can be used, as long as the boats can float while ferrying a candle.

- Find a launching site where there is easy access to water, perhaps a rockpool at the beach or a pond with gently shelving sides.

- Choose a very still evening for the launch of the boats as the slightest breeze will be enough to extinguish the votives. For best results, make the boats with sides, which will help to keep the wind off the candles.

- Remember to remove all boats and candles after the launch.

# HALLOWEEN FEAST

Halloween, October 31 , has been rather hijacked by the candy-hunting spooks and "trick-or-treaters," but in years gone by this date was a time to mark the end of autumn's harvest and the approach of winter. The first day of November was the Celtic New Year and celebrations began at dusk on the last day of October, when villagers gathered the best of the harvest for a great feast. This eve of the new Celtic year was believed to be a night when a gap opened between the world of the living and the world of the dead, and spirits were at large. Images of spirit guardians carved on turnips were placed on doorsteps to keep the evil spirits away, precursors of the pumpkin lanterns we make today.

## HOLDING A HALLOWEEN FEAST

For a magical Halloween, try holding a woodland feast lit by pumpkin lanterns to celebrate the end of autumn and the coming winter.

- Make the lanterns at home, using a selection of pumpkins. Cut the tops off the pumpkins with a sharp knife and then hollow them out, saving the flesh for soup or a pie and the seeds for roasting, to make a nutty flavored snack.

- Encourage the children to draw faces and patterns on the pumpkin skins, to provide a guide for carving. The skins are thick and tough so sharp knives must be used to cut the designs; children should only do this under very close adult supervision. Make sure the pumpkins are carved with plenty of holes so that the candles inside will get enough air to burn brightly.

- Once the pumpkins have been carved, place several votive candles inside each one.

- Choose a site for your picnic, perhaps in the garden, at a local park, or out in the woods. The ideal location is a forest clearing with tree stumps or logs to rest the lanterns on.

- Prepare a warming Halloween feast, such as hot baked potatoes, pumpkin soup, sausages wrapped in bread, toffee apples, or apple tarts—and perhaps some candy for those would-be trick-or-treaters!

- Perhaps the Halloween celebration could be a surprise party. Smuggle the pumpkins out to the chosen picnic spot and light them ahead of time. Then take the children outside, letting them suddenly come across the welcoming orange glow of the lanterns, arranged in a trail to lead them to an unexpected picnic in the woods or at the bottom of the garden.

- After the Halloween picnic the children could play a few games such as eating apples on strings or the feely boxes, bat and moth, or torch tag games (described in "Games to play in the dark," page 180).

## WHAT YOU NEED

Pumpkins of different sizes
Sharp knife
Pens/pencils
Votive candles
Seasonal foods
Apples threaded on strings or materials for other
games (see "Games to play in the dark," page 180).

## SAFETY TIPS

Supervise pumpkin carving closely as sharp
knives are needed to cut through the tough skin.
Never leave children unsupervised near lit lanterns.
Be very careful with candles in the woods; never
leave candles unattended and ensure you take
them all back with you.
Make sure all the children
are warmly dressed
in gloves and
boots.

# MOTH MYSTERIES

As darkness falls on a summer's night, multitudes of moths crawl out of their hiding places to fly off in search of nectar or a mate. Their sometimes-suicidal attraction to light means we most often see them in front of the car headlights or flying through an open window toward a lamp. These much-maligned creatures are usually considered rather a nuisance, but many moths are quite as beautiful as butterflies, and with their intricate markings and subtle coloring they are definitely worth a closer look.

The irresistible attraction that light has for moths will help children to trap them humanely and discover some of their mysteries. Moth-trapping is most successful on a warm, still, humid summer's night, in a garden near to an electricity supply. This activity should always be carried out under close adult supervision and in dry weather.

## MAKING A SHEET TRAP

A sheet trap attracts moths onto a white cloth under a bright light, but allows them to fly off whenever they wish.

• Hang an old white sheet over a washing line.

• Place a household lamp with a bare bright bulb in front of the sheet.

• Keep a close eye on the sheet to see how many different moths are attracted.

• If you have a large, bright torch, try setting up sheet traps in a variety of wild places, to see whether there is any difference in the number and variety of moths attracted.

## MAKING A BOX TRAP

Box moth traps are available in stores, but it is also easy for children to make a simple trap to use at home.

- An adult should use the scissors or knife to cut the plastic bottle carefully in half.

- Tear the lids off two or three egg boxes and fit the trays into the bottom half of the bottle along with a couple of pieces of scrunched-up kitchen roll. This will provide the moths with somewhere to hide, as well as making it harder for them to escape.

- Turn the top of the bottle upside down and place it into the base. This will act as a funnel down which the moths will slide into the base, where they can hide among the egg boxes.

- Take the trap outside and place it next to the light source. Direct the light so that it shines straight over the funnel-shaped top of the trap.

- Leave the trap outside for several hours, bringing both the trap and the light back indoors if it starts to rain.

- In the morning, open the trap carefully and transfer any trapped moths into a jar or a large bug box by allowing them to crawl on to a paintbrush. Do not touch them as their delicate wings are easily damaged.

- After looking at the moths, put them back in the trap and release them at dusk.

## MAKING A TREACLE TRAP

Have you ever wondered why some flowers emit a strong scent at night? They do this to attract moths, some of which have a keen sense of smell. Moths will be attracted to treacle smeared on a tree trunk or a post, and while they sip on the sweetness you can watch them in the light of a torch.

### WHAT YOU NEED

- A 8½-pint (5 litre) plastic bottle (of the type used for household cleaning liquids), thoroughly cleaned out by an adult
- Scissors/sharp knife
- Cardboard egg boxes
- Kitchen roll
- A household lamp with a bare, bright bulb
- Jars/large bug boxes
- Paintbrush
- Magnifying glasses and a simple field guide

### SAFETY TIPS

- Do not let children use electric lights unattended.
- Do not use electric lights outside when it is raining or in damp conditions.

179

# GAMES TO PLAY IN THE DARK

Many children love the excitement of playing outside after dark; my own childhood memories include torchlit games of tag, hide-and-seek and spying-on-the-grown-ups. Yet how many children in today's world are allowed to play outdoors after dark? Most parents call their children to come in as soon as the light begins to fade.

Residential school trips or events arranged by after-school clubs will offer opportunities for playing organized games in the dark. But families and friends can also take children outdoors to enjoy exciting games of manhunt, torch tag, or rope trails. There are also quieter games, which might involve listening to the sounds of the night or trying to identify mystery objects by touch.

### WHAT YOU NEED

**MANHUNT**
Glowsticks

**TORCH TAG**
- A blindfold, such as a scarf or eye-shades
- A torch

## MANHUNT

One dark night a glowstick trail led a group of rowdy boys deeper and deeper into the woods in search of adult quarry. The glowsticks had been placed carefully so the children would always see the next stick glowing up ahead. With strict instructions to stay together, the quickest boys waited at each glow-stick until everyone else had caught up. Even the most unruly child was a little anxious about getting lost, so the darkness encouraged the boys to stick together and work as a team. They soon discovered their quarry, leaping upon him in great excitement. Collecting all the glowsticks on the way home, the boys found other uses for them, throwing and spinning them wildly through the air.

## TORCH TAG

This game proved very popular at one of Jo's outdoor parties. Played in a forest clearing on a very dark night, it encouraged the children to use their listening and stalking skills and made them feel as though they were real secret agents.

- One child is blindfolded and equipped with a torch.

- The others are stationed in a circle around the blindfolded child; their role is to stalk their target by crawling along on their bellies through the undergrowth as quietly as possible.

- The blindfolded child listens very carefully and shines the torch in the direction of any noise. If the torchlight falls on a stalker, he or she has to stop still for thirty seconds before resuming the crawl.

- The game ends when the blindfolded child is captured.

- All the children must be offered a chance to use the torch.

## BAT AND MOTH

The bats we see swooping around after dark catch their prey using echolocation. They emit a series of very high-pitched sounds, which bounce back from any objects with which they come into contact. These signals are picked up by the bats' sensitive ears, allowing them to piece together an accurate picture of their surroundings and pinpoint any moving insects. Echolocation is used as the basis for this game, in which a blindfolded child plays the role of bat and another child acts as moth. Although the game can be played anywhere and at any time, it is more fun after dark, when the children might even see some real bats hunting for real moths.

- One person is chosen to be a bat and another a moth; everyone else stands around them in a circle, either holding hands or with arms outstretched.

- The bat wears a blindfold and seeks to find the moth by echolocation. This is done by calling out the word "bat," to which the moth must always reply "moth."

- The moth must respond each time the bat calls out, which helps the bat to build up a picture of where the moth might be found. The more frequent the calls (or signals, in the case of a real bat), the more the bat will know about the moth's whereabouts, even if the moth is moving around quite quickly.

- A successful bat needs to listen carefully and concentrate hard. A successful moth needs to move fast.

- The people in the circle do not provide any assistance other than helping the blindfolded bat to stay within the circle. They should be reasonably quiet so that the bat and moth can hear each other clearly.

- Once the bat has located and caught the moth, other children can have a turn at the game.

- You can make the game more complicated by having two moths at a time.

### FEELY BOXES

Imagine reaching into a box or bag, not knowing what might be lurking inside. Exploring fingertips tentatively feel an unknown object; perhaps it will be soft and slimy or rough and prickly or light and fluffy. You may know straightaway what you are touching or you may not be able to guess at all. This game is about identifying mystery natural objects by touch alone; it can be played in the dark or, in the daytime, with the help of blindfolds.

### WHAT YOU NEED

**FEELY BOXES**
- Box/bag/old pairs of tights
- Blindfolds, such as scarves or eye-shades
- A collection of natural materials

**ROPE TRAILS**
- Very long, sturdy ropes

### SAFETY TIPS
- Before playing night games, give the children a clear set of instructions about staying close together.
- Establish a central meeting point, which might be marked by a lantern.

- Make a collection of natural materials with different textures. This might include soil, leaf litter, a piece of rotting wood, an acorn, a holly leaf, a feather, some sheep's wool, a fir cone, or an empty snail shell.

- The materials should be put in boxes or bags, so that the children can feel them without seeing them. Alternatively, put each type of material in the foot of an old pair of opaque tights and secure with a knot.

- Sit the children in a circle and give each of them something to identify. Ask the children to describe the object they are feeling before saying what they think it might be. Can anybody guess the mystery items from the descriptions?

- At one party a feely box was balanced on a dad's knees. As a child reached into the box his hand was suddenly grabbed by the dad's hand, causing the child to jump and everyone else to laugh. Then they all wanted a go—not knowing quite when their hands might be grabbed!

## ROPE TRAILS

Blindfold rope trails, described on page 149, also work well in the woods at night, when it might be so dark that there is no need for blindfolds. The trail should be set up in the woods during daylight hours. Wind a long rope through the trees, at about the children's waist level. Choose a route with little or no undergrowth and no low branches. Then return after nightfall and encourage each child in turn to follow the trail through the darkness. There should be an adult at each end of the trail.

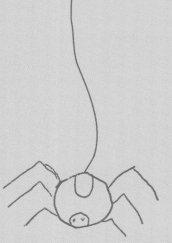

# FURTHER
# INFORMATION

# FURTHER INFORMATION

We hope this book will help to strengthen the relationship between children and wild places, and encourage families to discover more about the secrets and wonders of the natural world together. Wild places can be unpredictable, however, and sometimes a little frightening and occasionally dangerous. Let the children play and explore, but equip them with the knowledge they need to look after themselves and the environment. This section of the book offers tips on staying safe and minimizing damage to the wild places you visit, as well as suggesting some books, organizations, and Web sites that provide advice on getting families outdoors and further information about wildlife and the countryside.

## SAFETY RULES

For each and every outdoor expedition, keep in mind these ground rules about safety:

- Always take a basic first-aid kit to deal with cuts, bruises, and stings.

- Take a whistle and tell the children they should come back to you immediately if you blow it.

- Remind the children not to talk to strangers.

- Never let children play unsupervised near water.

- Don't let children use sharp tools such as knives or scissors unless they are being closely supervised.

- Don't let a group of children become too widely dispersed; encourage them to stay with a partner for activities such as wild tracking.

- Agree on a central meeting point where you can all gather at a prearranged signal.

- Tell the children never to eat wild foods unless a knowledgeable adult has told them it is safe to do so.

- Hands should be washed after playing outside.

## THE OUTDOOR CODE

Wherever you are going and whatever you are doing, use this code as a reminder of how to enjoy wild places while keeping damage and disturbance to a minimum. Remember that we have a responsibility to safeguard natural and semi-natural habitats so that future generations will also be able to enjoy them.

- Do not drop litter; always take all your trash home with you.

- Keep to marked paths where possible.

- Leave gates and property as you find them.

- Read and respect signs and notices.

- Avoid damaging buildings, fences, hedges, walls, and signs.

- Do not disturb nesting birds.

- Be gentle with any small animals you catch. Look at them carefully before returning them to wherever you found them.

- If you overturn a log to see what's underneath, turn it back afterward.

- Never uproot any wild plant. Only pick flowers that are both common and abundant.

- Try not to make loud noises, as this may disturb animals and birds.

- Guard against all risk of fire.

- Keep dogs under close control.

- Always have consideration for others; don't let children run wild and disturb other people's enjoyment of wild places.

- HAVE FUN!

## MAKING FIRES

The general advice about making fires in wild places is don't—the risks are just too high. However, as anyone who has sat around a campfire knows, they have a capacity to bring people together while making us feel closer to the natural world; and children are captivated by the magic of a campfire. There are a very few occasions when it is appropriate to make a fire outdoors. The fires photographed for this book were made either on the beach (during daylight) or at a friend's farm. Anyone wanting to enjoy the magic of a campfire should plan ahead, allow plenty of time, team up with someone with experience of making fires in the wild, and follow these safety rules:

- Always seek the landowner's permission.

- Never build fires during dry periods or when it is windy.

- Make sure you have plenty of water with you.

- Choose a quiet site where the fire won't impinge on others.

- Build the fire directly on mineral soil surrounded by an open area of bare ground with no exposed roots.

- Keep the fire as small as possible.

- Only use dead wood collected from the ground.

- Once all the wood has burnt to ash, pour water over it and allow it to cool completely. Scatter the ashes, and leave the site as you found it.

- For further details about campfires, refer to *Bushcraft* by Ray Mears.

# FURTHER READING

The following fiction and reference books might provide inspiration and information for natural explorers (see also other titles by the same authors). Many of the titles listed here were used as sources for this book.

## FICTION

Stories might be a starting point for all sorts of make-believe games and imaginary adventures. These examples of recent editions of classic and contemporary children's books might inspire games and activities in the natural world:

Burnett, Frances Hodgson, *The Secret Garden*, Puffin: London, 1994 (first published 1911)

Cooling, Wendy (ed.), *Earthwise: Poems About Our World*, Franklin Watts: London, 2000

Dahl, Roald, *The Magic Finger*, Puffin: London, 2004 (first published 1966)

Grahame, Kenneth, *The Wind in the Willows*, Walker Books: London, 2000 (first published 1908)

Lewis, C.S., *The Lion, the Witch and the Wardrobe*, Collins: London, 2000 (first published 1950)

Milne, A.A., *Winnie-the-Pooh*, Methuen: London, 2000 (first published 1926)

Nesbit, E., *The Railway Children*, Puffin: London, 1994 (first published 1906)

Paulsen, Gary, *Hatchet*, Macmillan Children's Books: London, 1991

Pitcher, Caroline, *The Snow Whale*, Frances Lincoln: London, 1996

Ransome, Arthur, *Swallows and Amazons*, Red Fox: London, 2001 (first published 1932)

Rosen, Michael and Oxenbury, Helen, *We're Going on a Bear Hunt*, Walker Books: London, 2001

Sendak, Maurice, *Where the Wild Things Are*, Red Fox: London, 2000

Tolkien, J.R.R., *The Lord of the Rings*, HarperCollins: London, 1999 (first published 1954–5)

## NONFICTION

Whether you are seeking inspiration or practical advice, the following books may help you with your natural exploring.

Cornell, Joseph Bharat, *Sharing Nature with Children*, Dawn Publications: Nevada City, 1998

Cox, Rosamund Kidman, *Usborne Complete First Book of Nature*, Usborne: London, 1990

Durrell, Gerald, *My Family and Other Animals*, Penguin: London, 1999 (first published 1956)

Edgington, Margaret, *The Great Outdoors*, Early Education: London, 2004

Einon, Dorothy, *Creative Play*, Penguin: London, 1986

Goldsworthy, Andy, *Time*, Thames and Hudson: London, 2002

Lister-Kaye, John, *Nature's Child*, Little, Brown: Boston, 2004

Manning, Mick and Granstrom, Brita, *Nature School*, Kingfisher: London, 1997

McManners, Hugh, *Outdoor Survival Guide*, Dorling Kindersley: London, 1998

Mears, Ray, *Bushcraft*, Hodder and Stoughton: London, 2002

Sample, Geoff, *Nature Safari*, Collins: London, 2003

Smith, Roly, *A Practical Guide to Country Walking*, Hamlyn: London, 1999

Thomson, John B., *Natural Childhood*, Gaia Books: London, 2000

Wilkes, Angela, *The Amazing Outdoor Activity Book*, Dorling Kindersley: London, 2001

Young, Geoffrey and Franks, Elaine, *Watching Wildlife*, George Philip: London, 1992

## FIELD GUIDES

If you and the children in your care would like to start identifying plants and animals, there is a wealth of field guides available. Good libraries and bookshops will offer a range of guides to suit all levels of interest and knowledge.

# USEFUL ORGANIZATIONS AND WEB SITES

The following organizations and Web sites provide advice on where to find wild places, as well as information about wildlife and the countryside.

## THE NATIONAL AUDUBON SOCIETY

www.audubon.org

This organization's mission is to conserve and restore natural ecosystems, focusing on birds, other wildlife, and their habitats, for the benefit of humanity and the earth's biological diversity.

## THE COUSTEAU SOCIETY

www.cousteau.org/en

The Cousteau Society, founded by Jacques Cousteau, is dedicated to the preservation of nature for future generations.

## EARTH DAY NETWORK

www.earthday.org

The Earth Day Network is a driving force steering environmental awareness around the world.

## NATIONAL GRASSLANDS

www.fs.fed.us/grasslands/index.shtml

The National Grasslands Visitor Center Web site details the 20 publicly owned, nationally recognized grasslands that total almost 4 million acres and are protected by the USDA Forest Service.

## THE NATURE CONSERVANCY

www.nature.org

The mission of the Nature Conservancy is to preserve the plants, animals, and natural communities that represent the diversity of life on earth by protecting the lands and waters they need to survive.

## THE NATIONAL PARK SERVICE

www.nps.gov

The National Park Service cares for national parks, a network of natural, cultural, and recreational sites across the nation. Visit this Web site for information on America's natural wonders from places like the Grand Canyon and Gettysburg to lesser known sites like Boston Harbor Islands in Massachusetts and Russell Cave in Alabama.

## THE SIERRA CLUB

www.sierraclub.org

The Sierra Club has been instrumental in preserving wilderness, wildlife, and nature's most splendid wild places for more than 100 years. It also helps to protect more than 150 million acres of wilderness and wildlife habitat.

## WORLD WILDLIFE FOUNDATION

www.worldwildlife.org

Since 1961 the World Wildlife Fund has worked to protect endangered species all over the world.

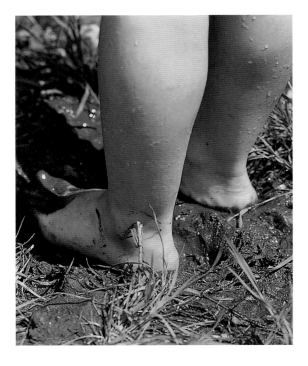

## INDEX

# ACKNOWLEDGMENTS

We could not have done this book without the help of the following children and their families: Lily, Toby, and Charlie; Edward and Carolyn; Cliffie, Frankie, and Anya; Sam; Francesca and Mattie; Jessie, Alice, and Johnnie; Bradley; Kristian; Felix, Rose, and Patrick; Jessica, Sophie, and Mac; Sam; Joey; Daisy and Oli; Kit; Harry; Ben; Carla, Louie, Stan, and Frankie; Anna and Mary; Lydia, Helena and Lucien; Patrick and Andrew; Matty and Tristan; Harry; Edward; William; Magnus; Fiona, Eliza and Genki; Jessica; Sienna and Christopher; Dachini, Djed and Yemaya; Chloe; Josh; Alexander; Chloe and Holly; Rose; Scarlett and Bluebell; Charlotte; Tom and Ellie; Ashley and Cameron; Millie, Hattie and Henry; Tom; Millie and Eva; Frances and Tim; Jim, Neil, and Evelyn; Faith and Edward; Anna, Ella, and Tim; Kate; Robert; William. Many thanks to all of them for their enthusiasm and patience. Our special thanks to Jake, Dan, and Connie, and to Hannah and Edward, for their sketches and for being such long-suffering models; and to Ben and Peter for their ideas and support. We would also like to thank each other—from the first germ of the idea right through to publication this has been a truly collaborative project.

The activities and ideas in this book come from a variety of sources; we would like to thank the children for their spontaneous suggestions and those friends who shared stories of their natural adventures with us. Some activities are old favorites, and others are drawn from my own experience of working in environmental education. Those books that provided us with inspiration and ideas are listed in "Further Reading" on page 188. Please notify the publisher if there have been any inadvertent omissions of acknowledgments and these will be rectified in future editions.

Finally, many thanks to everyone at Frances Lincoln who helped to make this book a reality.